Family Success

Family Success

By
Dr. Raymond Barber

SWORD of the LORD PUBLISHERS

P. O. Box 1099, Murfreesboro, TN 37133

Printed and Bound in the United States of America

CONTENTS

THE HOME WHERE CHRIST ABIDES

"And Jesus entered and passed through Jericho.

"And, behold, there was a man named Zacchæus, which was the chief among the publicans, and he was rich.

"And he sought to see Jesus who he was; and could not for the press, because he was little of stature.

"And he ran before, and climbed up into a sycamore tree to see him: for he was to pass that way.

"And when Jesus came to the place, he looked up, and saw him, and said unto him, Zacchæus, make haste, and come down; for to day I must abide at thy house.

"And he made haste, and came down, and received him joyfully.

"And when they saw it, they all murmured, saying, That he was gone to be guest with a man that is a sinner.

"And Zacchæus stood, and said unto the Lord; Behold, Lord, the half of my goods I give to the poor; and if I have taken any thing from any man by false accusation, I restore him fourfold.

"And Jesus said unto him, This day is salvation come to this house, forsomuch as he also is a son of Abraham.

"For the Son of man is come to seek and to save that which was lost."—Luke 19:1–10.

Christ makes the difference between a **house** and a **home**. In many homes there is a plaque on the wall that reads: "Christ is the Head of this home," or "Christ is the Lord of this house," or "Christ is the unheard Spokesman in every conversation and the unseen Guest at every meal."

Question: Is Jesus Christ really all of that to us? Does He mean **anything** to you, to your family, to your home?

Does He mean **everything** to you, to your family, to your home? I wonder sometimes if we just like the way that plaque looks, or we like the way the words sound. *Christ is the Head of this home*: is He really? How can we display such plaques when we seldom seek God's guidance, do not listen to Him speak or reserve a place for Him at the table?

A HOME THAT HAS UNDERGONE COMPLETE TRANSFORMATION

Christ changes people, circumstances and things. He makes the difference. There is a difference in having a guest in your home and having someone **abide** in your home. If all of your country cousins come over and announce, "We just want to visit with you for a day or two," you can put up with that. But for them to say, "We have come to live with you" is a different story.

Is Christ just a visitor in your home?

There is a difference in abiding and just coming as a visitor. Is Christ just a **visitor** in your home? If Christ **abides** there, then the family has undergone a complete transformation. I am not saying it has become perfect. Don't tell me you have a perfect husband; I have never seen one. Don't tell me you have a perfect wife; there is no such thing. Don't tell me your children are perfect; you know better! But we have a perfect Saviour who is constantly transforming, remaking, remolding and refinishing our broken lives.

Isn't it good that He knows how to transform us!

God's Word is the greatest commentary on God's Word. Pretend this is the first time you have ever heard this story:

"And brought them out, and said, Sirs, what must I do to be saved?

"And they said, Believe on the Lord Jesus Christ, and thou shalt be

2

saved, and thy house [thy household, thy family].

"*And they spake unto him the word of the Lord, and to all that were in his house.*

"*And he took them the same hour of the night, and washed their stripes; and was baptized, he and all his, straightway.*

"*And when he had brought them into his house, he set meat before them, and rejoiced, believing in God with all his house.*"—Acts 16:30–34.

That home underwent a total transformation. Something happened to that man that day that also happened to his family. Nothing good or bad can happen to us that doesn't affect our whole family. Be careful, because ultimately what you say or do will influence and affect every family member. When this jailor got saved, God did something for his family, for his household.

A home where Christ abides has undergone a complete transformation. Christ makes the difference between **existing** and **living**. Christ makes the difference between hell on earth and heaven in the confines of a home. Christ makes the difference between a **battleground** and a **playground**. Christ makes the difference between a war zone and a peace treaty.

> Christ makes the difference.

Observe Luke 19:9: "This day is salvation come to this house." The greatest thing that can happen to a family is Christ's coming into a home. Some of you may be expecting to win a sweepstakes with a ten-million-dollar check. It would be far better for Christ to come into your home than a check for ten million dollars.

You say, "But I could do a lot of church building with…" Hey, wait! It is not what you would do if riches were your lot; it is what you are doing with the dollar and a quarter you have. It would be far more beneficial to open the doors of your home, your heart, your lives. To say, "Come into our hearts, Lord Jesus. Be with us, bless us, abide with us, guide us, strengthen us, lead us, develop us, transform us by Your power," would do more than ten million dollars would do. And it will last for eternity!

"Believe on the Lord Jesus Christ, and thou shalt be saved, and thy house."—Acts 16:31.

"And the LORD said unto Noah, Come thou and all thy house into the ark."—Gen. 7:1.

Salvation is a family affair. Christ can transform the home.

GOVERNED BY BIBLICAL PRINCIPLES

There are many principles out in the world. All educational systems, philosophers, the economists, the environmentalists offer us principles by which to live. Every newspaper, every magazine, every television and radio program tell us "How to lose weight," "How to eat," "How to invest your money," "How to conduct the family," "Ten rules to happiness," and on and on. None begin to touch what the Word of God says. Every area of your business, your home, your schooling, your family, your life is addressed in the Word of God.

I wish to point out several areas where the Bible governs the way we live, the way we conduct our homes and families. The home where Christ abides is governed by biblical principles.

First, your diet and eating habits are governed by biblical principles—or should be. God is interested in the **body** as well as in the **soul**, because your body is the temple of the Holy Spirit. You live at such and such an address, and you are concerned about the looks of your house, concerned about the way it is heated and cooled, about the furniture.

Rightly so, because you live in it. But God lives in our bodies; therefore, He is concerned about where He lives. He wants it to be presentable inside and out. God desires our bodies to be healthy.

"What? know ye not that your body is the temple of the Holy Ghost which is in you, which ye have of God, and ye are not your own?

"For ye are bought with a price: therefore glorify God in your body, and in your spirit, which are God's."—I Cor. 6:19,20.

Food is essential. We read in Mark 5 about a little girl who had died. Jesus went into that home, touched that little girl and raised her up. Straightway He commanded that something should be given her to eat. Food is necessary. Your body is the temple of the Holy Spirit, and you ought to treat it as God's house because He lives in it. Be careful what you put in it. Eating right is important. Proper diet means a healthier body. See what Daniel 1:8–15 has to say about it:

"But Daniel purposed in his heart that he would not defile himself with the portion of the king's meat, nor with the wine which he drank: therefore he requested of the prince of the eunuchs that he might not defile himself.

"Now God had brought Daniel into favour and tender love with the prince of the eunuchs.

"And the prince of the eunuchs said unto Daniel, I fear my lord the king, who hath appointed your meat and your drink: for why should he see your faces worse liking than the children which are of your sort? then shall ye make me endanger my head to the king.

"Then said Daniel to Melzar, whom the prince of the eunuchs had set over Daniel, Hananiah, Mishael, and Azariah,

"Prove thy servants, I beseech thee, ten days; and let them give us pulse [some kind of bean] *to eat, and water to drink.*

"Then let our countenances be looked upon before thee, and the countenance of the children that eat of the portion of the king's meat: and as thou seest, deal with thy servants.

"So he consented to them in this matter, and proved them ten days.

"And at the end of ten days their countenances appeared fairer and fatter in flesh than all the children which did eat the portion of the king's meat."

If Christ is "the unseen Guest at our table," then we ought to eat properly. The home where Christ abides adheres to God's health laws.

Second, our work and responsibilities are governed by biblical principles. Work is ordained of God.

"And that ye study to be quiet, and to do your own business, and to work with your own hands, as we commanded you; That ye may walk honestly toward them that are without [the unsaved], *and that ye may have lack of nothing."*—I Thess. 4:11, 12.

Not only is it a good testimony to work, but it helps you to "lack...nothing." Here are more instructions about work and work responsibilities governed by biblical principles:

"Now we command you, brethren, in the name of our Lord Jesus Christ, that ye withdraw yourselves from every brother that walketh disorderly, and not after the tradition which he received of us.

"For yourselves know how ye ought to follow us: for we behaved not ourselves disorderly among you;

"Neither did we eat any man's bread for nought; but wrought with labour and travail night and day, that we might not be chargeable to any of you:

"Not because we have not power, but to make ourselves an ensample [or example] *unto you to follow us.*

"For even when we were with you, this we commanded you, that if any would not work, neither should he eat.

"For we hear that there are some which walk among you disorderly, working not at all, but are busybodies.

"Now them that are such we command and exhort by our Lord

Jesus Christ, that with quietness they work, and eat their own bread."—II Thess. 3:6–12.

"...that with quietness they work, and eat their own bread." The biblical principle is for us to work, for us to earn our living.

In the book of Ruth, we see that God took care of the poor. There was no welfare system. Please don't misunderstand me. Some people are certainly deserving of some help

We are to work and not depend on somebody else.

from whomever, but I am tired of paying taxes to feed people who won't work. God says, "If any would not work, neither should he eat." A biblical principle is laid out in the Scripture. We are to work and not depend on somebody else. It is a biblical principle that people work. No work, no eating, the Bible says.

The home where Christ abides adheres to God's instruction about earning a living.

Third, budgeting your money and making your investments are governed by biblical principles. Luke 19:8 says, "Behold, Lord, the half of my goods I give to the poor." The first thing this guy did after meeting Jesus was to start giving. Many people who are saved are selfish, but Christians should not be selfish because they are "Christ-ones." Since Christ is unselfish, Christians should be unselfish. "Behold, Lord, the half of my goods I give to the poor; and if I have taken any thing from any man by false accusation, I restore him fourfold." When the spirit of the Saviour comes in, the spirit of selfishness goes out, and the greedy "getter" becomes a gracious giver.

This man had just met Jesus. He had never been to Sunday school, nor had he attended a stewardship banquet, nor had he heard anybody talk on stewardship and giving; but he said immediately, 'I am going to give half of my goods away, and if I have taken anything by false pretenses, I am going to restore it fourfold.' That is the spirit of Christ. That is the spirit of giving.

Drink in every word of this passage in Matthew 6:19–34 and listen to what God says. Get the principle for yourself.

"Lay not up for yourselves treasures upon earth, where moth and rust doth corrupt, and where thieves break through and steal:

"But lay up for yourselves treasures in heaven, where neither moth nor rust doth corrupt, and where thieves do not break through nor steal:

"For where your treasure is, there will your heart be also.

"The light of the body is the eye: if therefore thine eye be single, thy whole body shall be full of light.

"But if thine eye be evil, thy whole body shall be full of darkness. If therefore the light that is in thee be darkness, how great is that darkness!

"No man can serve two masters: for either he will hate the one, and love the other; or else he will hold to the one, and despise the other. Ye cannot serve God and mammon.

"Therefore I say unto you, Take no thought for your life, what ye shall eat, or what ye shall drink; nor yet for your body, what ye shall put on. Is not the life more than meat, and the body than raiment?

"Behold the fowls of the air: for they sow not, neither do they reap, nor gather into barns; yet your heavenly Father feedeth them. Are ye not much better than they?

"Which of you by taking thought can add one cubit unto his stature?

"And why take ye thought for raiment? Consider the lilies of the field, how they grow; they toil not, neither do they spin:

"And yet I say unto you, That even Solomon in all his glory was not arrayed like one of these.

"Wherefore, if God so clothe the grass of the field, which to day is, and to morrow is cast into the oven, shall he not much more clothe you, O ye of little faith?

"Therefore take no thought, saying, What shall we eat? or, What shall we drink? or, Wherewithal shall we be clothed?

"(For after all these things do the Gentiles seek:) for your heavenly

Father knoweth that ye have need of all these things.

"But seek ye first the kingdom of God, and his righteousness; and all these things shall be added unto you.

"Take therefore no thought for the morrow: for the morrow shall take thought for the things of itself. Sufficient unto the day is the evil thereof."

What on earth is Jesus saying? In a nutshell, the most important thing in life is not what you are going to wear, what you will eat, what you have, or what you possess. The most important thing is laying up for yourselves treasures in Heaven.

Put first things first. If God clothes the lily, feeds the raven—and you are much more important than ravens and fields of clover and lilies that blossom and bloom in the spring—don't you think He will supply your needs? Don't you believe that He will take care of you?

> **Put first things first.**

What was Jesus saying? Don't be worried; don't spend all your time thinking what you are going to do next week or what you are going to do next month or what you are going to do next year. "Sufficient unto the day is the evil thereof."

Jesus taught His disciples to pray, "Give us **this day** our daily bread"—not next week, not tomorrow, not next year. You are thinking, *Does Dr. Barber think it is wrong to have a savings account?* Absolutely not! *Does he think it is wrong to save for a rainy day?* No! Go out and buy an umbrella! What I am saying is, get the proper perspective. Put God first, seek first His kingdom, invest in Heaven and in heavenly things; and God will add all these other things.

We can't rightly invest the ninety percent until we have first invested the ten percent. When dealing with God's money, you can't invest it in something else and expect Him to pay dividends. So the principle is, put your money first in God's business, then trust Him to feed you, to give you wisdom to lay aside some money for college or for your children. Get the proper perspective. Give God a chance to help you with those other things that He said He would help you with.

There is the principle; now abide by it. If Christ abides in the home, surely you can put Him first in your financial planning.

Consider the law of giving and getting. Luke 6:38 says: "Give, and it shall be given unto you; good measure, pressed down, and shaken together, and running over, shall men give into your bosom. For with the same measure that ye mete withal it shall be measured to you again." This principle will help your family be more stable, more solid, more productive financially. If these principles do not work, then Christ did not know what He was talking about.

You say, "But that was two thousand years ago; He didn't know about this inflation." Oh yes, He did. God didn't wake up this morning and say, "Oh, dear Me! Inflation is rising. People are losing their jobs. I didn't know that was going to happen." No. God knows all about what is going on. He knew what this year was going to bring your way. He wasn't surprised at what happened to you last week. He knows what the inflation rate is; He knows what the CD rate is. If these principles don't work, Jesus Christ didn't tell the truth, or He was mistaken and didn't know what He was talking about.

> God's program of economics begins with the word *give*.

God's program of economics begins with the word *give*. A commitment to biblical stewardship will produce financial freedom and stability. Try it and see. The home where Christ abides puts God first in financial planning.

Fourth, lifestyle and entertainment are governed by

biblical principles. The greatest enemy of the home is secular humanism. Television programs are full of it. Talk show programs are brainwashing people. Can you believe some of the things you hear? And when you watch a commercial advertising the pictures and the programs for next week, there is a sawed-off shotgun right in your face on the television screen.

During the Persian Gulf War, I heard some so-called psychologists say: "Don't let the children look at those war pictures. It will warp them." That is strange, isn't it, when they can see more in a commercial than they saw in the war pictures? They have seen more people blown up in commercials than they saw in the entire Persian Gulf War.

Secular humanism, violence and secularism are ruining our children. Parents, learn how to control the television set. It is easy for you to push the children off to the den and say, "Now watch television. This will keep you quiet while we are doing so-and-so." You should govern what they watch because so much of it is poison, it is brainwashing, it is sex, it is violence, it is homosexuality right out there just as blatant as can be—things that fifteen or twenty years ago we wouldn't have dreamed would have been on television. If it keeps going like it is, in ten more years there will be scenes of absolute nudity and the sex act right on the main channels.

Our children are exposed to violence six to eight hours a day (that is the average), then we wonder why these kids pack their pistols to school and shoot each other—and the teacher. We need not wonder. We know why: television is brainwashing them with secular humanism—"live high, die young, have a good time while it lasts, there is no higher power, there is no God." Humanism is coming in subtly in education and in television, and it is destroying America. It all comes in the form of entertainment.

It is so sad what we allow to entertain us. What has

happened to "ring around the rosies," "hide and seek" and picture puzzles? Why do we have to sit before a big television screen to be entertained? What has happened to the family's coming together and sitting around the table talking? What has happened to conversation? Why don't we get back to that? Why don't we get back to some plain, simple ways of entertainment?

Kids, do you know what used to entertain us? (You are going to laugh at this!) We would find ourselves tin cans, stomp them, one with each foot, then walk down the street kicking the tin cans so they would make a little noise! Or we got a metal rim and rolled it down the street using a stretched-out clothes hanger to guide it. Or we found an old rubber tire and rolled it down the street. Or we balled up a Coke paper cup, rolled it as tight as we could, and played ball with it by hitting it with a stick.

What has happened to just plain, simple, family entertainment, with parents sitting around and telling their children stories from yesteryear or reading books to them? I can tell you what has happened. We have become so busy, so selfish, so self-centered, so concerned about what the neighbors are going to think and trying to keep up with the Joneses, we have lost our children, our families and our basic family-oriented values. We have allowed Hollywood to brainwash us. We think we can't go to sleep without watching a television program where somebody is flaunting homosexuality or some form of so-called entertainment. Where have our Scripture-based, family-oriented values gone?

God's admonition for us is:

"The night is far spent, the day is at hand: let us therefore cast off the works of darkness, and let us put on the armour of light.

"Let us walk honestly, as in the day; not in rioting and drunkenness, not in chambering and wantonness, not in strife and envying.

"But put ye on the Lord Jesus Christ, and make not provision for the flesh, to fulfil the lusts thereof."—Rom. 13:12–14.

In Galatians 5:16-26 God tells us what our lives should be:

"This I say then, Walk in the Spirit, and ye shall not fulfil the lust of the flesh.

"For the flesh lusteth against the Spirit, and the Spirit against the flesh: and these are contrary the one to the other: so that ye cannot do the things that ye would.

"But if ye be led of the Spirit, ye are not under the law.

"Now the works of the flesh are manifest, which are these; Adultery, fornication, uncleanness, lasciviousness,

"Idolatry, witchcraft, hatred, variance, emulations, wrath, strife, seditions, heresies,

"Envyings, murders, drunkenness, revellings, and such like: of the which I tell you before, as I have also told you in time past, that they which do such things shall not inherit the kingdom of God.

"But the fruit of the Spirit is love, joy, peace, longsuffering, gentleness, goodness, faith,

"Meekness, temperance: against such there is no law.

"And they that are Christ's have crucified the flesh with the affections and lusts.

"If we live in the Spirit, let us also walk in the Spirit.

"Let us not be desirous of vain glory, provoking one another, envying one another."

Biblical admonitions on Christian lifestyle and on wholesome entertainment are in II Corinthians 6:14–18. These principles should govern our lives:

"Be ye not unequally yoked together with unbelievers: for what fellowship hath righteousness with unrighteousness? and what communion hath light with darkness?

"And what concord hath Christ with Belial? or what part hath he that believeth with an infidel?

"And what agreement hath the temple of God with idols? for ye are the temple of the living God; as God hath said, I will dwell in them, and walk in them; and I will be their God, and they shall be my people.

"Wherefore come out from among them, and be ye separate, saith the Lord, and touch not the unclean thing; and I will receive you,

"And will be a Father unto you, and ye shall be my sons and daughters, saith the Lord Almighty."

The home where Christ abides engages in wholesome activities.

First, the home where Christ abides has undergone a complete transformation; second, it is governed by biblical principles; and third, it is

ASSURED OF EARTHLY HAPPINESS AND HEAVENLY BLISS

You can have happiness on earth right now. Happiness is in the home where Christ abides. Psalm 1 starts out with the word *blessed.* Literally it is rendered *hilarious.*

"Blessed is the man that walketh not in the counsel of the ungodly, nor standeth in the way of sinners, nor sitteth in the seat of the scornful.

"But his delight is in the law of the LORD; and in his law doth he meditate day and night.

"And he shall be like a tree planted by the rivers of water, that bringeth forth his fruit in his season; his leaf also shall not wither; and whatsoever he doeth shall prosper.

"The ungodly are not so: but are like the chaff which the wind driveth away.

"Therefore the ungodly shall not stand in the judgment, nor sinners in the congregation of the righteous.

"For the LORD knoweth the way of the righteous: but the way of

the ungodly shall perish."—Ps. 1:1–6.

For a treatise on happiness on earth and joy in Heaven turn to Revelation 19:1–9:

"And after these things I heard a great voice of much people in heaven, saying, Alleluia; Salvation, and glory, and honour, and power, unto the Lord our God:

"For true and righteous are his judgments: for he hath judged the great whore [that is, the religious system, the Babylonian system], *which did corrupt the earth with her fornication, and hath avenged the blood of his servants at her hand.*

"And again they said, Alleluia. And her smoke rose up for ever and ever.

"And the four and twenty elders and the four beasts fell down and worshipped God that sat on the throne, saying, Amen; Alleluia.

"And a voice came out of the throne, saying, Praise our God, all ye his servants, and ye that fear him, both small and great.

"And I heard as it were the voice of a great multitude, and as the voice of many waters, and as the voice of mighty thunderings, saying, Alleluia: for the Lord God omnipotent reigneth.

"Let us be glad and rejoice, and give honour to him: for the marriage of the Lamb is come, and his wife hath made herself ready.

"And to her was granted that she should be arrayed in fine linen, clean and white: for the fine linen is the righteousness of saints.

"And he saith unto me, Write, Blessed are they which are called unto the marriage supper of the Lamb. And he saith unto me, These are the true sayings of God."

If you don't think God is going to make us happy in Heaven, then just listen to the "alleluia," the praise to God. By the way, don't be so starchy and stiff; praise God once in awhile.

Turn back to the text, Luke 19. Look at what Jesus said to Zacchæus in verse 5: "…for to day I must abide at thy house." If by some miraculous event Jesus stood outside your door and said, "I must spend the night in your house," would you say, "Lord, could you give one more day? Make it tomorrow night? Some things I have to get out of the magazine rack; I must clean up my VCR; I need to get some things out of the refrigerator." Jesus said, "To day I must abide at thy house." That is sobering, isn't it?

A home where Christ abides has undergone a complete transformation, is governed by biblical principles and is assured of a happy life on earth and eternal bliss in Heaven.

How spiritual is your home?

GOD'S APPRAISAL OF CHILDREN

"And they brought young children to him, that he should touch them: and his disciples rebuked those that brought them.

"But when Jesus saw it, he was much displeased, and said unto them, Suffer the little children to come unto me, and forbid them not: for of such is the kingdom of God.

"Verily I say unto you, Whosoever shall not receive the kingdom of God as a little child, he shall not enter therein.

"And he took them up in his arms, put his hands upon them, and blessed them."—Mark 10:13–16.

Someone has wisely said, "No man ever stood so tall as when he stooped to help a little child."

In these days of widespread abuse and wholesale molestation of children, we should be on guard and do all that is within our power to preserve and protect this most prized possession—our children.

Have you ever wondered what home would be like without little fingerprints all over the place? Love them while you have a chance. Pray with them while you can. Before long they will be gone from your tender, loving care. If you do not plant the seed of the Word of God in their hearts while they are young, pliable, teachable and tender, the Devil will plant other things there. Don't think any family is immune to the poisonous venom of Satan. Satan strikes in the most righteous camps, in the most godly homes. Where it is least expected, he comes and takes his toll.

The poet penned:

God wants the boys, the merry-hearted boys,
The noisy boys, the funny boys, the thoughtless boys.
God wants the boys with all their joys,

That He as gold may make them pure
And teach them trials to endure.
His heroes brave He'd have them be,
Fighting for truth and purity.
God wants the little boys.

God wants the happy-hearted girls,
The loving girls, the best of girls, the worst of girls.
God wants to make the girls His pearls,
And so reflect His holy face,
And bring to mind His wondrous grace,
That beautiful the world may be
And filled with love and purity.
God wants the little girls.

Surely we need to raise an umbrella of loving care over them. Jesus stood tall when He took a little child upon His lap and held him in His arms. Here is an amazing thing about Jesus Christ: He was so stern and strong that He drove the money changers out of the temple with a whip, yet so tender, so mild, so meek, so gracious, so loving, so compassionate and so full of concern that even little boys and girls could feel secure in His arms. What a wonderful Saviour is Jesus Christ our Lord! Jesus highly esteemed the little boys and the little girls.

Jesus loves the little children,
All the children of the world;
Red and yellow, black and white,
They are precious in His sight;
Jesus loves the little children of the world.

CHILDREN MUST BE BROUGHT TO JESUS IN ORDER TO RECEIVE HIS BLESSING

There is no other way little ones can receive the blessings that Jesus Christ has for them except for somebody to bring them to Him. Look again at verse 13: "And they brought young children to him." We don't know their names. If you are a servant of Christ, it is not important what your name is. If you love the little children, your name doesn't have to appear in the church paper every week or on the bulletin board. We don't know the names of these people, but somebody brought them to Jesus. In spite of the opposition, in spite of the risk they had to take, they brought young ones to Christ.

Bring them in spite of opposition. Not everybody wants little children to come to know Jesus Christ. The perpetrators of pornography don't want little children to know about Jesus. The operators of sin dives of the world don't want it. It takes away from their business. Many a man has sold his soul to the Devil for one more dollar, and it didn't matter how he made it. On the streets of San Francisco, Los Angeles, Dallas, Fort Worth, New York City, Atlanta, Miami, ten-year-olds and twelve-year-olds are peddling drugs. Drug pushers don't want little children to come to know Jesus; but you and I should be willing to pay the price, go the second mile, do whatever is necessary, to bring them to Jesus.

Consider the bus ministries. Thousands more little children could be brought to Sunday school if more adults really cared. Only a few go out on Saturday to visit and enlist them. That is a sad commentary on you who sit in the pews and are not willing to sacrifice a couple of hours on Saturday and a couple on Sunday to invest in the souls of our most priceless treasure—the little boys and girls. People are sitting on church pews who ought to be driving church buses, or having a bus route, or being bus captains, or teaching Sunday school. The children's ministry may not always seem to be the most rewarding job in the world. You have to give up something, you have to care, in order to do it. But tell me what is more important than rescuing boys and girls from street gangs! You think the street gangs are all in Los Angeles? No, they are everywhere.

Do we really love?

Shame on you who are just warming a bench, you who are not willing to get out and rescue some boys and girls from the thorns of sin!

JESUS WELCOMES CHILDREN

Children are always welcomed by Jesus. He never turned a little one away. Isn't it strange that Jesus took them into His **arms**, and we want to put them in the **corner**?

> Children are always welcomed by Jesus.

When Jesus saw that the disciples rebuked those who brought little children to Him, verse 14 tells us, "…he was much displeased and said unto them, Suffer the little children to come unto me, and forbid them not: for of such is the kingdom of God."

Sunday school teachers, bus workers, never think you are spending your time in vain. It may seem that you are getting nowhere; that you are not getting through to them; that they don't listen nor understand. You can't see it, but God is putting something in their hearts.

Jesus always welcomes little children. Do you?

JESUS HIGHLY VALUES CHILDREN

Children are highly valued by Jesus. In verses 15 and 16 Jesus said, "Verily [absolutely, truthfully] I say unto you,

> Children are highly valued by Jesus.

Whosoever shall not receive the kingdom of God as a little child, he shall not enter therein." What is more innocent than a little child?

And by the way, they act about like Mama and Daddy act. If Mother and Daddy eat garlic, don't expect the children to come up smelling like roses. The fruit falls close to the tree. As the twig is bent, so grows the tree. Daddy and Mother are reflected in son and daughter.

Verse 16 says, "And he took them up in his arms, put his hands upon them and blessed them." Can't you imagine what a feeling that must have been when the Son of God, whose hands carved out the mountains, scooped out the oceans, and hung the stars in place, touched those little bodies! What a blessed thing it would have been to have been able to have sat on His lap and heard Him say, "Suffer the little children to come unto me, and forbid them not: for of such is the kingdom of God"!

Jesus highly valued the little ones and even rebuked His own disciples for attempting to restrain them.

BRING THEM TO JESUS AT AN EARLY AGE

Children should be brought to Jesus at an early age by their parents. It is sad that many parents are not concerned and are not willing to pay the price. If it were not for a few bus workers, some children would never get to hear the Word of God because their parents have partied all night and are still asleep when the bus pulls up in front of the house. Sometimes bus workers have to go in and get the children ready. They wash their faces and see that they get a bite to eat.

I remember a few years ago I knocked on a door in the neighborhood near the church I pastored and said to a little boy, "I want you to come to Sunday school. Will your mother and daddy let you come?"

He answered, "Mister, I ain't got no daddy, and my

mother doesn't love me anymore." Such a story could be told a thousand times over in most any city.

I say to you parents, bring them while they are young. The Bible says these children who were brought to Jesus were very young. Jesus took them up in His arms. Three-fourths of all of those who come to Christ are brought to Him at an early age. Statistics will prove that most of those saved are saved before they are 15 years old. What are the odds? 5,000 to 1 that anybody will get saved between ages 18 and 25. The odds increase between ages 25 and 35, to 25,000 to 1. Between ages 35 and 45, it is 80,000 to 1; and between ages 45 and 80, one million to one. You had better get them saved while they are young. Children are God's apostles sent forth day by day to preach love, hope and peace.

FOUR WAYS YOU CAN BRING YOUR CHILDREN TO JESUS CHRIST

1. By maintaining a beautiful Christian environment in the home. Children watch **examples** far better than they listen to **preaching**. If your home is an armed camp, don't expect your children to be peaceful. If you sit around and criticize the church, the pastor, the youth leaders and the church program, don't expect the children to do anything but criticize. What they hear at home is what they are going to repeat. If they hear you pray, they will learn to pray; if they hear you gossip, they will learn to gossip; if they hear you criticize, they will learn to criticize. If they are brought up in an environment of bickering and fussing, feuding and fighting, they will bicker and fuss and feud and fight. But if you bring them up in a beautiful Christian environment, you stand a much better chance of getting them into Heaven.

2. By maintaining consistent family devotions. Turn off the television a little early at night and gather the children around and pray with them. You see that they get the best in education, wear the best clothes, eat the best food, go to places where they get intellectual stimulation. You give them money and teach them to save it for their college education. Yet you deprive them of the most priceless thing that you could give them: a few moments a day in the Word of God and in prayer.

Don't expect them to act like angels at church if they have seen you act like a devil at home. Don't expect them to have a desire to learn the Word of God if you don't share it with them in family devotions. What a tragedy for a young girl or boy to grow up having never heard Daddy or Mother pray. Oh, they have heard you talk about everything else—football, basketball, baseball, handball, kickball, race cars, Hollywood, television, picnics, parties! They have heard you talk about the weather, about the president, about the governor, the mayor, politics, government, education, business, money and banking—but they have never heard you talk about Jesus. You had better have family devotions while you can influence them, because the day is coming when they will be gone from you and it will then be too late.

3. **By maintaining a concerted effort to teach biblical principles.** You teach them how to brush their teeth, how to comb their hair, how to wash their dirty ears and feet, how to put on their clothes and how to get their lessons. Then why not teach them the principles of righteousness, sobriety, honesty and purity based on the Word of God?

4. **By maintaining a record of faithful church attendance.** It is not just a darting in and out and wondering, *What is it going to be today?* Some people come to church, fold their arms and say, "Okay, Preacher, I am here; now entertain me." It is not his business to entertain you. The church is

> The church is not an entertainment center.

not an entertainment center; it is a preaching center.

Parents with a spasmodic, irregular church attendance record cannot expect their children to fall in love with Jesus, the Sunday school or the church. Attending only when it is convenient or when there is a special program is not going to get the job done. Children need to see you in church every Sunday. Consistency in your life is most important.

Parents, how do you grade yourself on these four ways you can bring your children to Jesus Christ?

Do you talk to God about your children and then talk to your children about God? The only earthly possessions that you parents can take to Heaven are your children. Oh, I appeal to you in the name of Jesus Christ, make sure that all your children are saved. The poet wrote:

Are All the Children In?

I think ofttimes as the night draws nigh
　　Of an old house on the hill,
Of a yard all wide and blossom-scarred,
　　Where the children played at will.
And when the night at last came down,
　　Hustling the merry din,
Mother would look around and ask,
　　"Are all the children in?"

'Tis many and many a year since then,
　　And the old house on the hill
No longer echoes to childish feet,
　　And the yard is still, so still.
But I see it all as the shadows creep,
　　And though many the years have been,
Even now I can hear my mother ask,
　　"Are all the children in?"

I wonder if when the shadows fall
　　On the last short earthly day,
When we say good-bye to the world outside

And all tired with our childish play,
When we step out into the other land
    Where Mother so long has been,
Will we hear her ask as we did of old,
    "Are all the children in?"

I wonder also what the Lord will say;
    Will He say to us as older children of His,
"Have you cared for the lambs? Have you
        shown them the fold?"
    A privilege, joyful it is.
And I wonder, too, what our answer will be
    When His loving questions begin:
"Have you heeded My voice? Have you told
        of My love?
    Are all My children in?"

PARENTAL INFLUENCE IN FAMILY LIFE

"And the LORD *said, Shall I hide from Abraham that thing which I do;*

"Seeing that Abraham shall surely become a great and mighty nation, and all the nations of the earth shall be blessed in him?

"For I know him, that he will command his children and his household after him, and they shall keep the way of the LORD, *to do justice and judgment; that the* LORD *may bring upon Abraham that which he hath spoken of him."*—Gen. 18:17–19.

How would God characterize your parental program? Would God say about you, "I know him; I know her; I know them. I know they will bring their children up in the fear and admonition of the Lord. I know that they are going to instill in their children the basic principles that I have laid down in My Word. I know that they are going to set an example, that their children will know that the church is important, the Bible is true, Heaven is real, the Holy Spirit is their companion, Jesus Christ is their Saviour, and that only principles based on the Word of God are strong enough, good enough and pliable enough to instill in their hearts"?

Could God say that about your role as a parent? Or will you offer Him this excuse, "Well, now, dear God, You know when I was a child I was abused, so I am going to abuse my children"? or, "Dear God, You know when I was a child, we didn't have anything going for us, and so I don't think I ought..."? Don't try to put that off on God; He knows better. Just because some psychologist suggests that because somebody was abused when he was a child, he is justified in beating, bruising, battering and hurting his children or somebody else's, that doesn't make it true, reasonable or acceptable. I am sick and tired of people's going on talk

27

shows across the nation and saying, "Well, this happened to me, so I guess it is just natural that I have to take it out on somebody else." That is not God's prescription.

Abraham was not always in a godly environment. God called him out of a pagan country. If you didn't grow up in a Christian home, don't excuse yourself by saying, "Well, I can't provide Christian principles, Christian conduct, a Christian example and a Christian model because I didn't have it when I was a child." That is inexcusable.

The most important relationship is our relationship to God through Jesus Christ. Nothing transcends it, nothing is equal to it, nothing can substitute for it. But next in importance to this **eternal** relationship is the **earthly** relationship among members of the same family. Nothing is more refreshing than a family living together in harmony, unity and oneness. Mothers and fathers who fail to see the value of establishing a warm, personal, loving, lasting relationship with their children are indeed blind.

The keynote in this family relationship is **love**, and where love **controls**, children are **controlled**. That doesn't mean they will never make a mistake or that they will never go wrong. But when they are loved, the total program of their lives will be under the control of the one who loves them. The strongest tie that binds is the tie of love. Building such a loving relationship is a guaranteed prescription for building character in children.

Someone has defined *character* as "doing the right thing, at the right time, in the right way, for the right reason, with the right attitude." Character-building doesn't start when children are twelve or eighteen years old. It begins at birth and is a lifelong process. It takes many years to grow an oak, whereas one can produce a squash in a few weeks. The most effective building block that parents can use is setting a proper, godly example before their children.

PARENTAL ROLE MODEL NECESSARY

Almost without exception every child will pick out somebody about whom he will say, "When I grow up, I want to be like that person." Young people, be careful in select-

> Children need role models after which to pattern their lives.

ing your role model. The wrong one will steer you in the wrong **direction** and lead you to the wrong **destination**. Do not choose a sleazy, sexy, sensual, Hollywood character. Do not choose a foul-mouthed, dirty-joke-telling television comic. Do not choose a wild-eyed, drug-using, irreverent rock star. Do not choose a beer-guzzling, so-called "safe-sex" advocate, even if he is a super sports figure. Choose someone with Christian character and Christian values after whom to pattern your life.

Concerned, caring, compassionate parents have a greater influence on children than any other role model in the world. The influence of Mother and Daddy upon the children is greater than that of the pastor, the youth leader, the Sunday school teacher, the schoolteacher, any public figure or public hero.

Children do not expect their parents to be perfect, but they have every right to expect them to be honest, up-front and fair in dealing with them. It is the divine provision that children take almost twenty years to grow up, to develop into mature adults. No fifteen- or sixteen-year-old knows more than his parents, regardless of how smart he thinks he is or she thinks she is. Young people, just because you have been brought up in a different age, a different society, a different world than your parents and have been exposed to things that they were not exposed to, don't think you are smarter than they are. Don't think you know everything because you are now a teenager. Parents know far more than you do about how long you ought to stay out at night, with whom you ought to associate and not associate, how you ought to dress, how you ought to speak and think and walk and talk. I admonish you to listen to them.

During the formative years of growing up, parents must set a good example in being morally pure, spiritually strong and socially acceptable. **Give your children spiritual anchors while they are in the harbor so they will not sink when they encounter the storm at sea.** And they will meet the storms.

I mention five anchors:

The anchor of love.

The anchor of faith.

The anchor of hope.

The anchor of respect for authority.

The anchor of basic moral values within the framework of the Judeo-Christian ethic and culture in which we live.

You cannot afford to be without these anchors. You ought to instill these ideals in, and attach these anchors to, your children. Drop these anchors from their lives so that when they get out there on the sea, and the storms and the temptations are raging against them, they will be secured steadfastly by these anchors.

> **Children learn more at home than anywhere else.**

Children learn more at home than anywhere else. After all, their minds are more pliable; they are more teachable in the early years of their lives when their parents have them hour after hour, day after day, week after week, month after month, and year after year.

They learn their basic manners at home. If they embarrass you when you go out to eat, they are just mimicking you, in most cases. If they pull the tablecloth up and wipe their mouths on it, they have probably seen somebody at home do that. Somebody set before them an example, and it wasn't the president, the governor, nor the mayor. They learn basic manners, basic values and basic behavioral patterns at home.

There is no substitute for godly parents, Christian homes and family togetherness.

CHILDREN TEND TO EMBRACE SAME PHILOSOPHY AS THEIR PARENTS

Here is a principle: A child is usually an echo of his parents. Children will in most cases accept their parents' philosophy. Generally speaking, a parent's religion becomes the child's religion; a parent's politics become the child's politics; a parent's attitude usually becomes the child's attitude; a parent's beliefs usually become the child's beliefs. As a rule, a child will not only act but will react in somewhat the same manner as his parents act and react.

If you eat onions and garlic, don't expect the children to smell like roses. They will act the same way as you politically, religiously, educationally, socially and psychologically. If a child grows up with criticism, he will be critical. If a child grows up with quarreling, he will quarrel. If a child grows up with bitterness, he will be bitter. If a child grows up with anger, he will be angry. If a child grows up with cursing, he will curse. If a child grows up with selfishness, he will be selfish. If a child grows up with hypocrisy, he will be hypocritical. If a child grows up with cynicism, he will be cynical. If a child grows up with sensuality, he will be sensual. If a child grows up with deceit, he will be deceitful.

On the other hand, if a child grows up with compassion, he will be compassionate. If he grows up with kindness, he will be kind. If a child grows up with consideration, he will be considerate. If a child grows up with meekness, he will be meek. If he grows up with honor, he will be honorable. If he grows up with honesty, he will be honest. If a child grows up with truth, he will be truthful. If a child grows up with purity, he will be pure. If he grows up with love, he will be loving. As the twig is bent, so grows the tree.

Parents, do your children really have respect for you, for your judgment, for the principles that you try to teach them, for the way in which you are trying to guide them? Children will put faith and confidence in you only to the degree that they respect you: little respect, little confidence; little respect, little faith.

Parents, heed this warning: Be careful that you do not lose the respect of your children. Sometimes you wonder why they aren't doing as you say do. Sometimes the reason is that they have lost respect for you.

Let me name several things that will cause you to lose the respect of your children:

1. **Creating a credibility gap.** If you are not truthful with them, they will lose respect for you. The same is true in your dealings with your mate, your friends, your church, your pastor and your neighbors. If there is a credibility gap, you are done for. You might as well hang it up.

2. **Hypocritical behavior.** Nobody wants to follow a hypocrite. Someone comes by unexpectedly to visit. You fling the door open and say, "Come in; I am so glad to see you!" Then later you say before your child, "Why on earth did she come and mess up my day and take up my time?" Your child was sitting there observing your hypocritical behavior. A lot of children are wavering because they have seen the hypocrisy of their parents.

3. **Having a double standard will cause parents to lose the respect of their children.** Having one standard at church and another standard at home won't work. Don't be partial

in discipline, taking it out on one child and letting the other get by with no discipline. Both children will grow to disrespect you. Don't show partiality and unfair measures of punishment. You wouldn't use a steam roller to run over a gnat. Why then would you use an unreasonable punishment when something much lighter would work?

4. **Broken promises**. You promise a child, "We will do it at three o'clock," or "We will do it tomorrow," or "We will do it tonight," then you don't do it. The barometer of your respect has fallen a hundred degrees with one broken promise. If you don't intend to keep a promise, don't make it. Broken promises have caused many a child to lose absolute and total respect for Mother or Daddy. It might seem like a little thing, but what seems like a little thing to you and me is something big to a child.

5. **Lack of discipline.** The lack of discipline is probably as devastating as anything else to destroy the respect that your children have for you.

Children need to be disciplined; they expect to be disciplined and are disappointed when they are not. They lose respect for a parent who will let them get by with just about anything. You are producing a rebel for society when you let that happen. If he wants to tear the wallpaper off the wall, some people think, *I don't want to warp him by correcting him.* Later on, he goes downtown to the store and rips the pictures off the wall. He ends up in jail, and they wonder why. It all goes back to the time they let him tear the wallpaper off the wall because they didn't want to disturb his growing personality. If you say, "I don't want to hurt my little one; I don't want to repress his desires," you will see the day when he will cast that right into your teeth.

You say, "My child will love me because I have never whipped him." Shame on you! I have never seen a child that didn't need a good spanking once in awhile. If you want to lose your children's respect, then withhold discipline, withhold punishment, withhold correction. That will cause them to lose respect for you more quickly than anything else. 'Spare the rod and spoil the child.'

CHILDREN MUST HAVE PARENTAL AMMUNITION TO FIGHT THE ENEMIES

The **sensual nature of the flesh** is one enemy. Galatians 5:17–21 reads:

"For the flesh lusteth against the Spirit, and the Spirit against the flesh: and these are contrary the one to the other: so that ye cannot do the things that ye would.

"But if ye be led of the Spirit, ye are not under the law.

"Now the works of the flesh are manifest, which are these; Adultery, fornication, uncleanness, lasciviousness,

"Idolatry, witchcraft, hatred, variance, emulations, wrath, strife, seditions, heresies,

"Envyings, murders, drunkenness, revellings, and such like: of the which I tell you before, as I have also told you in time past, that they which do such things shall not inherit the kingdom of God."

The sensual nature of the flesh must be corralled, disciplined and put in order. Every person is susceptible to every one of the things Paul mentions. If we allowed the flesh to take its flight and do unrestrained what it wanted to do, most of us would be involved in most of these sins.

Another enemy is the **subtle influences of the world.** First John 2:15–17 reads:

"Love not the world, neither the things that are in the world. If any man love the world, the love of the Father is not in him.

"For all that is in the world, the lust of the flesh, and the lust of the

eyes, and the pride of life, is not of the Father, but is of the world.

"And the world passeth away, and the lust thereof: but he that doeth the will of God abideth for ever."

If you parents don't warn, advise and counsel your children about the subtle influences of this world, you are going to lose them. Humanism is the most subtle "religion" in all the world. (It was declared a "religion" by the Supreme Court of the United States of America.) In public school rooms all over America, we can hang up any kind of code of ethics as long as it is not Scripture. But as you know, it is illegal to have the Word of God in schools. "You can't bring that in; wait until children get in jail; they can read it in there," they say. Public schools can't put the Ten Commandments up, but they can put up some code of some ancient sage.

Humanism has subtly taken over public education in America. There are some exceptions, but generally, public education has been taken over by humanism. The humanists say, "If we have to have a god, we will be our own god. We don't believe in anything supernatural. It is all natural, all earthly, all here, all now. There is nothing hereafter—no accountability, no reporting to anybody." This humanistic, godless, atheistic philosophy is eating away at the core of Christian values in America.

Sexual promiscuity is another one of those subtle influences of the world. Did you ever think that you would live to see the day when condoms would be passed out to school children; that they would be taught to have sex as long as it is "safe sex"? Try abstention; that is the safest route, God's route; that is the Bible way, the only way. I cannot believe what I see on television and read in the newspapers about what is happening in the public school system and in our society. What is America coming to? Where is America headed? Is not the judgment of God hanging heavily over us?

How would a parent ever get his son or daughter not to do drugs while he sips his beer? One of the most damnable drugs we have in America is **alcohol.**

Rock music is destroying our children. I wish we could get rid of all rock music, with its subtle, sensual messages. Don't even classify it as music. It is noise.

The **scheming tactics of the Devil** are another enemy. Ephesians 6:12 says, "For we wrestle not against flesh and blood, but against principalities, against powers, against the rulers of the darkness of this world, against spiritual wickedness in high places." Satan is a schemer, sin is subtle, and many people are being deceived by persuasive advertising and powerful propaganda. Television is the propaganda tool in America with its brainwashing, propagandizing, making things look so good, so beautiful, so bright, so promising and so enjoyable. But they don't put up the last frame—the slimy hand of Satan wrecking and ruining and destroying. Many homes are under satanic attack, and many parents seem to be unaware of what is happening to their children.

Parents, you ought to know where your children are, what time they leave, what time they come home, with whom they go, with whom they come back, what they take out, and what they bring back. Don't be so busy gaining profit and popularity that you lose touch with reality. Your children should come first. It is more important for you to make them a **life** than it is to make them a **living.**

The following are three of the things that parents can do to exert proper influence on their children:

1. Make sure that their values are biblically oriented.

"Finally, brethren, whatsoever things are true, whatsoever things are honest, whatsoever things are just, whatsoever things are pure, whatsoever things are lovely, whatsoever things are of good report; if

there be any virtue, and if there be any praise, think on these things."—
Phil. 4:8.

2. Make sure that their lifestyle is godly.

"I beseech you therefore, brethren, by the mercies of God, that ye present your bodies a living sacrifice, holy, acceptable unto God, which is your reasonable service.

"And be not conformed to this world: but be ye transformed by the renewing of your mind, that ye may prove what is that good, and acceptable, and perfect, will of God."—Rom. 12:1, 2.

3. Make sure that you stand courageously against all sinful, subtle, satanic influences directed against your children.

"Wherefore take unto you the whole armour of God, that ye may be able to withstand in the evil day, and having done all, to stand.

"Stand therefore, having your loins girt about with truth, and having on the breastplate of righteousness;

"And your feet shod with the preparation of the gospel of peace;

"Above all, taking the shield of faith, wherewith ye shall be able to quench all the fiery darts of the wicked.

"And take the helmet of salvation, and the sword of the Spirit, which is the word of God."—Eph. 6:13–17.

I relate the stories of two families:

The Family of Max Jukes

Max Jukes, who lived in the state of New York, did not believe in Christian training and married a girl of like character. From this union, 1,026 descendants have been studied: 300 were sent to the penitentiary for an average of 13 years each; 190 became public prostitutes; 100 were drunkards.

On today's economic scale, the family cost the state over six million dollars. There is no record that they made any positive contribution to society.

The Family of Jonathan Edwards

Jonathan Edwards, who resided in the same state, believed in Christian training and married a woman of like mind. From this union, 729 descendants have been studied: 300 became preachers of the Gospel; there were 65 college professors, 13 university presidents, 60 authors of good books, 3 United States Congressmen, and one vice-president of the United States.

It is impossible to estimate the contributions this family made to the state of New York and to the country. The Edwards family is a sterling example of the biblical principle: "Train up a child in the way he should go: and when he is old, he will not depart from it" (Prov. 22:6).

Parental influence makes the difference. Since Max Jukes and his wife did not have the proper influence over their children, they produced rogues and thieves and prostitutes and bank robbers and drunkards. The Jonathan Edwards family produced college professors and preachers and bankers, a vice-president and congressmen.

There is no influence like parental influence. The church cannot do it, the schools cannot do it, the clubs cannot do it, organizations cannot do it. It has to be done in the framework of the family. Some of you have tried hard, and in spite of what you have done, you have wayward sons and daughters. I commend you to the grace of our Lord Jesus. Don't give up, but hold on, keep on praying, keep on trusting, keep on believing, keep on hoping, keep on doing, keep on going, because God is still on His throne and He is still in control. He brought a prodigal out of a hogpen, and nothing is impossible with Him.

Parental influence makes the difference in family life.

ROLE OF FATHER IN THE HOME

If the fathers of our nation would fulfill the role of fathers, our nation would be a better nation, churches would be better churches, homes would be better homes. Fathers, there is a tremendous responsibility upon your shoulders. God is holding you accountable.

"And the LORD said to Samuel, Behold, I will do a thing in Israel, at which both the ears of every one that heareth it shall tingle.

"In that day I will perform against Eli all things which I have spoken concerning his house: when I begin, I will also make an end.

"For I have told him that I will judge his house for ever for the iniquity which he knoweth; because his sons made themselves vile, and he restrained them not.

"And therefore I have sworn unto the house of Eli, that the iniquity of Eli's house shall not be purged with sacrifice nor offering for ever.

"And Samuel lay until the morning, and opened the doors of the house of the LORD. And Samuel feared to shew Eli the vision.

"Then Eli called Samuel, and said, Samuel, my son. And he answered, Here am I.

"And he said, What is the thing that the LORD hath said unto thee? I pray thee hide it not from me: God do so to thee, and more also, if thou hide any thing from me of all the things that he said unto thee.

"And Samuel told him every whit, and hid nothing from him. And he said, It is the LORD: let him do what seemeth him good."— I Sam. 3:11–18.

Not every man who fathers a child biologically is in the true sense of the word a father. Physically he is. It is one thing to be capable of producing offspring; it is another thing to be a *father*.

I am going to give you my description of a real dad: **A real dad is caring, compassionate, considerate, concerned, conscientious; he is capable of establishing a warm, loving, lasting relationship with his children who, in turn, are proud to call him "Daddy."**

I don't know why a golf game, an antique show or a trip to wherever would be more important to you than fulfilling your spiritual responsibilities. Children do not need a super-man or a macho image, but they do need a strong, masculine father figure in the home. Your children do not demand **perfection**, but they do demand and deserve **performance.** Your children do not need heavy-handed brutality, but they do need a hearty measure of discipline. Here is the bottom line: they need to see in you a balanced blend of **masculine toughness** and **spiritual tenderness** that springs from a heart of genuine concern for their well-being.

In the text, we have a perfect example of a derelict father, a prime example of a father who made the team but fumbled the ball. Remember the sins of his sons. Instead of punishing them, Eli pampered them. He failed to restrain his boys. Look again at verse 13: "For I have told him that I will judge his house for ever for the iniquity which he knoweth; because his sons made themselves vile, and he restrained them not."

God is going to punish Eli's household. He is going to make it plain that there will never be a sacrifice for this man's sins. Eli failed to carry out the father role in his home that he should have. He failed to discipline his boys. He failed to order his household after God's plan and program. Eli's sin as a father was not immorality, not burglary, not lying, not cheating. His sin was a lack of parental restraint and discipline. God judges that kind of behavior.

Because of the breakdown of discipline and restraint in Eli's home, the whole nation of Israel suffered a breakdown in morality and godliness. The consequences? Eli died an old, fat man with a broken heart and broken neck.

"Now Eli was ninety and eight years old; and his eyes were dim, that he could not see.

"And the man said unto Eli, I am he that came out of the army, and I fled to day out of the army. And he said, What is there done, my son?

"And the messenger answered and said, Israel is fled before the Philistines, and there hath been also a great slaughter among the people, and thy two sons also, Hophni and Phinehas, are dead, and the ark of God is taken.

"And it came to pass, when he made mention of the ark of God, that he fell from off the seat backward by the side of the gate, and his neck brake, and he died: for he was an old man, and heavy. And he had judged Israel forty years."—I Sam. 4:15,16.

God brought judgment upon Eli for failing to discipline his children.

I give you a solemn warning: Fathers, don't let this happen to you and to your children. Seek the face of God; discover the will of God; learn the way, the work, the plan of God for your home. Don't pull down the restraints. If you say, "But they are only children once so I will let them do anything they want to do," you are writing a prescription for misery, death, destruction, judgment and annihilation from God.

The failure of men to be the right kind of fathers has resulted in a breakdown of the American home. In most cases, what is wrong in the American home today is a father who hasn't fulfilled his role according to the Word of God. The breakdown in the home has led to chaos and confusion.

Do you wonder why there is rebellion in school? Because of rebellion in the home. Do you wonder why there are riots in Los Angeles, Dallas, Atlanta, Phoenix, Fort Worth and other places? Because there have been riots in the home.

There is not an area of national life in America today where there aren't many problems—economically, politically, socially, governmentally, educationally and religiously. Much of it goes back to the lack of parental restraint and discipline.

If you fathers will dedicate yourselves to Jesus Christ, will seek divine counsel in operating your homes and will establish biblical principles in your families, this nation could have a great spiritual awakening. I cannot emphasize enough the importance of ordering your family in the ways of the Lord.

There are three things I want to discuss with you fathers:

THE RIGHT RELATIONSHIP WITH GOD

A good father has a right relationship with God.

A father who does not know the love of God cannot love his children with a godly love. A Christian father has benefits that an unsaved father doesn't have.

There is the benefit of **prayer**. Isn't it wonderful to see a Christian father bring his children together and pray with and for them? An unsaved father can't do that. Here is a tragedy: Many *saved* fathers are not doing that, and that is to their own detriment and shame.

There is the benefit of **getting wisdom from God**. The unsaved man cannot get wisdom from God to teach his children in the ways of the Lord, but a saved man can. A Christian father can get wisdom to incorporate Christian principles and ideals in his whole program of life. An unsaved father cannot do that. A Christian father can lead his children to an altar of prayer and there dedicate them to God. An unsaved father cannot do that.

I ask these questions: Are you in the right relationship

with God? Do you know Jesus Christ as your own personal Saviour? Do you walk daily with God? As a father in the home, do you feel the responsibility and mandate from a righteous God to set the proper example? Or have you said, "Well, I tried but it didn't work, so I have just turned it over to the wife"? God didn't turn it over to the wife; He turned it over to you! God is not looking to the wife to order the home.

Please don't misunderstand me. In fatherless homes, the wife has to play the role of the authority figure. I am talking about homes where there are men whom God has given at least a grain of sense to know how to bring up children in the right way. You have a real problem if you have turned it over to Grandma and to the wife and to the state and to the church and to the Sunday school. God expects fathers to do it. Are you in the right relationship with God?

THE PROPER EXAMPLE

I am talking about vital areas like godliness, integrity, morality, attitudes and honesty. Those **little,** dishonest things that your son or daughter sees you do will become

> **A good father sets the proper example.**

big, dishonest things after awhile. Sin never remains little. Your children can pick up the attitude you have toward their mother even if you never say a word. They know how you feel about her. You don't have to say to them, "I'm sick of your mother. I don't want to live with her any longer." They don't even have to hear you scold her. It just comes by osmosis. It seeps out of you and into them without your ever putting on a demonstration. They pick up on your attitude toward the church, toward the pastor, toward the neighbor, toward your friends and toward your boss. You can't hide it.

Consistency is a word we need to practice. You can't do one thing at church and another thing at home. Many parents wonder five or ten years later, *Why aren't our children going to church anymore?* I know why. They had roast preacher for dinner every Sunday. They got spiritual indigestion, and Rolaids will never overcome it. They have seen you set two standards. You criticized the song leader, the pastor, the church. You criticized the sincerity of other Christians, saying they were phony—and the children have believed you. Now you can't get your children anywhere near the church because you put a critical attitude in front of them.

If you will **practice** holiness and not just **preach** it, you will not have to **demand** the respect of your children: you will have **earned** it! If they see in you the same person at home that they see when you sing in the choir, preach a message or teach a class; if they see the same conduct, same attitudes, same behavior, you won't have to demand their respect; you will have already earned it.

THE RIGHT PRIORITIES

God made the father the head of the family. The family is a body, and as goes the head, so goes the body.

> A good father has the right priorities.

Let me illustrate. My head wants to go to some physical point. My body says, "Well, if the head is going, I am going too." So my body just follows my head. What am I trying to say? As the head of your family, you take your children everywhere you go.

In the priority of provision, providing the best in education is important. Providing the best in social adjustment is absolutely necessary. Providing the best in financial security is commendable. But nothing is as important as providing the very best in **spiritual** development for your children.

Here is something I have never been able to understand: Fathers will see that their children go to school every school day for twelve long years to develop their minds, but they won't see that they are in Sunday school twelve months to develop their souls. That is strange to me because the soul will live forever.

It is important to provide the very best in spiritual development.

Fathers, lead your children to trust Christ. Teach them the Word of God. Anchor them to the church. Their future destiny largely depends on you. It is either Heaven or Hell, and you can make the difference. The most important priority is spiritual relationships.

A loving, caring father will never do or say anything to lessen his children's faith in God, in the church or in the pastor. A caring, compassionate, loving father will faithfully participate in the ministries of the church. A caring, compassionate father will consistently support the church financially.

I want to ask you a question: Who do you think built the church and the Sunday school rooms? Somebody's tithe did it to train your children. A caring, loving, compassionate father who is in the right relationship with God will do all in his power to build his children's respect for the house of God, the Word of God, the work of God, the people of God and the man of God.

I fear this is where it all breaks down. A family without family devotions has neither a roof over its head nor a foundation under its feet. If children know their daddy depends on God, they will depend on God. If your children observe you seeking God's wisdom and guidance, they will seek God's wisdom and guidance. If your children hear you pray, they will pray. Someone wrote,

> When Father prays the house gets still;
> His voice is slow and deep.
> We shut our eyes; the clock ticks loud,

So quiet we must keep.

When Father prays he doesn't use
    The words the preacher does.
There's different things for different days,
    But mostly it's for us.

Sometimes the prayer gets very long
    And hard to understand;
And then I wiggle up quite close
    And let him hold my hand.

I can't remember all of it;
    I'm little yet, you see.
But one thing I cannot forget:
    My father prays for me.

I would rather have a daddy that prayed for me than a
daddy that was a millionaire ten times over. The fondest
memory I have from my childhood is not when we went to
the park and played, but when I heard Daddy pray. I never
heard any man pray like him. Sunday mornings down in the
basement of our house, I could hear him. He could wake up
the household when the Spirit of God came on him! Then
when he came to the pulpit, the people knew he had been in
the closet with God.

Oh, that we had more praying daddies! You don't have
to be a theologian to pray, nor a pastor, nor have much education. All you have to do is get the little family together and
say, "We are going to talk to God this morning," and then do
it. Some people worry, "I can't pray an hour." You don't have
to pray an hour—when alone, maybe, but not while the family has gathered together. Don't make them recite the Ten
Commandments every morning. Don't make them memorize fifteen chapters every day. They will turn against it if
you are not careful. Simply be a good example.

I am recommending three things for every father to do regarding the children:

> **Dedicate** them to God.
> **Discipline** them wisely.
> **Develop** them spiritually.

POSITIVE POINTERS ON PARENTAL PERFORMANCE

"Children, obey your parents in the Lord: for this is right.

"Honour thy father and mother; which is the first commandment with promise;

"That it may be well with thee, and thou mayest live long on the earth.

"And, ye fathers, provoke not your children to wrath: but bring them up in the nurture and admonition of the Lord."—Eph. 6:1–4.

The business of establishing proper family relationships is a two-way street. Paul admonishes children to be obedient unto their parents. That is absolutely essential for harmony in the home, order in the nation and peace in the world. On the other end of that spectrum, Paul says to fathers and mothers, "...provoke not your children to wrath: but bring them up in the nurture and admonition of the Lord."

God made man in His own likeness and image. We, as God's creatures made in His likeness and image, are somewhat like Him, and He is somewhat like us. God has given duties and responsibilities where duties and responsibilities belong. God has charged parents with accountability where accountability belongs. All of God's creatures are accountable to Him.

> All of God's creatures are accountable to Him.

God has given many gifts to the human race. He started out in the Garden at Eden. The greatest gift God can give to a husband and wife is a child. Life, we believe, begins at conception. Therefore, we must guard against any measures that would destroy prenatal life. When God gives the precious gift of a child, He brings about one new life composed of two separate lives. This results in Mother and Daddy's having a common interest in their offspring. Their roles are similar, while simultaneously different in some respects. God has entrusted them with an awesome responsibility of joint custody of their children. Daddy must not put it all off on Mother; Mother must not assign it all to Daddy. Father leads the way, and Mother follows the pattern that is set. God's composition of the family is father, mother, child (or children) working together, and I emphasize **together**. You cannot pit your child against your spouse and expect God to bless your program in life. Working together, you can develop your children into mature, responsible individuals capable of making a significant contribution to society. This can best be done when **divine instructions** are followed.

The Bible is our "how-to" Book. I am not against some of the programs of child training that I have read, but there is no improvement on what God says about it. Doesn't it make sense that if God created us, He can give us wisdom to know how to operate our lives? If God gave you a child, doesn't it make sense that He can tell you how to bring up that child in the right way and under the right circumstances? It doesn't take a million dollars nor a college education. I suppose these might be helpful in some cases, but we wouldn't know what to do with a million dollars, and many wouldn't know how to handle a college education. God has equipped you. To those who lack wisdom, James says, "If any of you lack wisdom, let him ask of God, that giveth to all men liberally, and upbraideth not; and it shall be given him" (1:5). God gives us wisdom from His wisdom Book.

Parents, you ought to read the book of Proverbs, a chapter a day. God will give you wisdom. Bringing up children and making them significant contributors to the world around them can best be done by following divine instructions and by incorporating wise measures.

These are difficult days. Our children and young people

are being pulled away from us. There are centrifugal forces that will pull them out of your jurisdiction. The Devil will swoop them up; he will swallow them up; he will destroy them if he possibly can. That is why it is important that we stay within the framework of God's Word.

Let me give you seven "Positive Pointers on Parental Performance."

MORAL AND SPIRITUAL VALUES

Parents should instill moral and spiritual values in their children at an early age.

"And these words, which I command thee this day, shall be in thine heart:

"And thou shalt teach them diligently unto thy children, and shalt talk of them when thou sittest in thine house, and when thou walkest by the way, and when thou liest down, and when thou risest up."—Deut. 6:6,7.

One of the most notorious infidels and agnostics this nation has ever produced was Tom Paine who said it was in the first five years of his life that he became an infidel. The most formative years of your child's life are the first five or six years. The Catholics said it a long time ago, something like this: "Give us a child until he is six, then you can teach him anything you want to, but he will stay with the Catholic doctrine." You know that has just about been true, if you know anything about Catholicism. God does not leave us without admonition and instruction. Proverbs 22:6 says, "Train up a child in the way he should go." When he is ten, twelve or fifteen years old, it is probably too late. Training has to begin in the cradle.

> **Training has to begin in the cradle.**

Let me caution you parents: Maintain a balance in your

spiritual training and instruction and in your religious training and religious instruction. There are two extremes: an
overkill and an **underkill**. Many are underkilling, that is, just
skimming over it, getting by with what they can and not
really going very deep in training their children. Then there
are those who are on an overkill. Don't expect Johnny to
memorize the first twenty-five chapters of Genesis by the
time he is two. Don't demand that he read the Bible six
hours a day or pray four hours. Set a sane, sensible program.
You know better than anybody else what it takes.

Here is something to think about. One day our nation is
going to be taken over, conquered by a numberless army.
This vast army will control every area of public and private
life. It will control government from the precinct to the pres-
idency; it will control all communications systems; it will
control the military; it will control college and education; it
will control industry; it will control commerce; it will control
travel; it will control Wall Street; it will control business,
banking and financing; it will control the economy; it will
control politics; it will control religion and education; and it
will control you and me.

Right away you ask, "Who on earth is this army that has
such great potential and such great power?" The answer is
simple: It is none other than the vast army of children who
are growing up around us. In time, if Jesus Christ tarries His
coming, these children and young people will be in total
control of everything.

Let me give you a stern warning: If this vast army of
children is not taught moral and spiritual values while they
are young, imagine what kind of world we will have to live
in tomorrow—in the days and years that should be our
golden years of retirement. Just think what it will be like in
the next generation if this generation now growing up is not

disciplined, trained and brought up in the fear and nurture and admonition of the Lord.

Chaos and confusion will be the order of the day. Fear, failure and frustration will supremely reign. We will be destitute, disgraced and demeaned if this vast army does not receive proper instruction. Parents, face reality:

• Those sweet, tender, little lips that bubbled out "goo-goo" to you from the cradle will either bless God or curse man.

• Those little feet, precious little feet that you covered up with those beautiful little booties, will one day walk generously and graciously on errands of mercy, or they will march in riots and demonstrations.

Put enough garbage in, and garbage will come out. Unless we control what children watch on cable and on the major stations of television, they will get more garbage than we can ever clean out of them.

Parents, don't make the den a classroom and the television a teacher. There are few programs that are fit for children or even adults to watch. Most corrupt, drag down, brainwash and poison the mind.

Someone has said, "That little hand that you squeezed so tightly to lead safely across the street, will one day hold a gun or hold a Bible."

The Sunday schools, the private schools, the public schools, the boys' clubs, the girls' clubs—all combined can never do for your children what your home can do for them. The home is the vanguard for truth and morality in child-training. There is no substitute for home training. If they don't get it there, they won't get it anywhere.

How foolish we are! Think about this: Engineers, architects and builders with a corporate mandate will spend thousands of hours and millions of dollars to make certain a ship is seaworthy before they cast it out into the angry waters of the sea. But most parents will spend very little time, very little energy, very little effort, very little money to build character into their children to make sure that they are "seaworthy" before they cast them out onto an angry ocean out there in life. It is sad that men care more for ships and cargo than we do for siblings and children! Where are we going? What is the next generation going to be like? So many young people, as they launch out into life—whether it be college or career or marriage or something else—are unprepared and untrained.

Parents, instill moral and spiritual values in your children while they are young.

A SENSE OF BELONGING

> **Parents should cultivate a sense of belonging in their children.**

Can you imagine in thirty-five years of pastoring in one church how many homes I have gone into and seen written across the faces of little children, "Nobody loves me." They haven't all been heathen homes either. Many have been church people's homes where the parents have been so busy making a dollar or so busy partying and satisfying themselves that they have neglected their own children. Sadly enough, they have depended on the Sunday school to correct their mistakes or the preacher to take over and make their children everything they ought to be.

Psalm 127:3 says, "Lo, children are an heritage of the LORD: and the fruit of the womb is his reward." Children are God's gifts to you. Let's give them **hugs**, not **drugs**. It is absolutely foolish, insincere and cowardly for a father to warn his child of drugs while he is sipping beer. "I just want to be a social drinker so I can fit in with my peers. I have to stay in good standing with my boss, and I have to make contacts." Ever hear that? Let me tell you something: your peers, your boss, your contacts will admire you more if you say "no." You can make a sale without a glass of beer, a glass of wine, or a glass of liquor in your hand. The trouble is that you want it.

Hugs, not drugs; love, not license; parameters, not permissiveness. If your children feel they don't belong to you, it won't be long before they find someone else to whom they can feel they do belong.

LISTEN TO YOUR CHILDREN

Parents should take time to listen to their children. Look at Genesis 22:7, 8:

"And Isaac spake unto Abraham his father, and said, My father: and he said,"

"I don't have time right now, Son. Don't be asking me questions. Go ask your mother"; or, "You will learn when you get a little bit older." Is that how it reads? No, Abraham said,

"Here am I, my son. And he said, Behold the fire and the wood: but where is the lamb for a burnt-offering?

"And Abraham said, My son, God will provide himself a lamb for a burnt-offering: so they went both of them together."

What if Abraham had ignored his son's question? He would have lost a golden opportunity to teach him a wonderful lesson on faith. Abraham said, 'Son, don't worry about it; God will provide Himself a lamb.'

Someone has estimated that the average child will ask 500,000 questions by the time he or she is fifteen years old.

You had better start listening to about 499,000 of them. Pay attention to the questions your children ask. It provides you with an opportunity to teach them wholesome lessons of biblical truth and moral values.

A child says to his father, "Daddy, what are we going to be like in Heaven?" His father answers, "I don't have time to answer your question now. Can't you see I'm busy? Ask your Sunday school teacher." In turning his son or daughter away that daddy is missing the best opportunity of his life to tell that child where Heaven is, how to get there, how to be saved, and what we are going to be like. All he has to do is turn to I John 3:2 and show him, "…we shall be like him; for we shall see him as he is."

Don't turn a deaf ear to his questions. After all, asking questions is a way to learn. Listen to him while he is young, and he will listen to you when he gets older.

DEVELOP THEIR TALENTS
AND ABILITIES

> Parents should encourage the development of special talents and abilities in their children.

The 18th chapter of Matthew has often been called the child's chapter because in several of the verses Jesus addresses the children. "Take heed that ye despise not one of these little ones [one of the most amazing statements that Jesus ever made]; for I say unto you, That in heaven their angels do always behold the face of my Father which is in heaven."

After reading that verse for fifty years, it just dawned on me what it really means. Jesus probably was drawing from a local setting. (He did a whole lot of that.)

One day He talked about a man going forth to sow.

Since every one of them had seen farmers out sowing, they knew exactly what He was talking about.

He talked about a loaf of bread; He talked about a little flower; He talked about the rain; He talked about the clouds; He talked about the sun. He drew all of His teaching from things around Him. Jesus took the simple and made it sublime.

Here is from where I believe Jesus was taking this: In the Roman world, royal children of royal families had tutors. Look at Galatians, chapter 4, where Paul talks about tutors, guardians and messengers. Children in that day had tutors who were guardians appointed by the father until a child was a certain age. That guardian had access to the father of that child when nobody else did.

Now, watch the application. Jesus said, 'In Heaven, all of these little children have a messenger, an angelic representative.' They are right before the face of the Father, and God will stop everything He is doing in the universe to listen to one of those messengers representing one of His little children. Isn't that amazing? "Their angels do always behold the face of my Father which is in heaven." God gives them special attention because they are representing special people.

Your children are special, so recognize and develop the talents and abilities that you discover in them. When you observe a spark of creativity, cultivate it, whether it is in music, art, poetry or some other area. Sadly enough, many a child has gone through life frustrated because his parent failed to detect a special talent or didn't take time to develop it. That is a tragedy, isn't it? Reward your children when they excel. Praise them for a job well done. Be generous with your compliments. Why, even a mosquito gets a pat on the back when he does a good job!

Do not show partiality in praise. All children do not have the same talent or temperament. So don't expect the

> **Don't expect the same thing out of each of your children.**

same thing out of each one of them. They are different. No two snowflakes are alike. Be very careful never to praise or reward one child to the neglect of another. Haven't you seen it happen in families, that one child got all the attention, all the praise, all the compliments, while the others were neglected and, consequently, were warped for life? Don't build up one to the detriment of another. Don't do anything for one at the expense of another. Be fair and impartial in your treatment. Don't expect the same thing out of each of your children. They are individuals, they are different, and they are not going to produce the same thing.

GIVE THEM QUALITY TIME

> **Parents should spend quality time with their children.**

Ephesians 5:16 says, "Redeeming the time, because the days are evil." Take time to laugh and play with them. Proverbs 17:22 reads, "A merry heart doeth good like a medicine: but a broken spirit drieth the bones." How many little children have been pushed away when they wanted to play because their parents were too busy! Take time to relax. Take time for fun and fellowship. You don't have to go to a famous amusement park. Take them on a picnic. Play a game of sandlot ball. Go on a fishing trip. Take them to the zoo. Drive them to the ice cream parlor or better yet, to the yogurt shop! You don't have to have an organized activity. You don't have to have a party and invite a hundred people. You don't have to fly off to Orlando, San Francisco, Los Angeles, Phoenix, Dallas or somewhere. Just right at home have a little playtime with the children. Let them pretend home is an amusement park. Have everyone look in the mirror, and let them pretend it is the zoo!

Someone took a survey among three hundred children, and this is what he came up with: The average time spent with them by their fathers

> **Childhood comes only once.**

was **seven and a half minutes a week!** "Oh, but," you say, "you don't understand. I have so many business deals to take care of." Let me tell you something, buddy. Business comes again next week, next month, next year, but childhood comes only **once.**

TEACH THEM RESPECT FOR AUTHORITY

One fundamental problem in America is a lack of respect for authority, demonstrated by acts such as people's calling the policemen "pigs." Any company that would put out a record, a song or a tape sug-gesting the harming of a police-man or anybody else ought to be shut down. I am for the police department. I know there are some

> **Parents should teach their children respect for authority.**

policemen who don't always do right. But there are some plumbers who don't always do right, some preachers who don't always do right, some painters who don't always do right. Even some parents don't always do right. But I will sup-port the "blue," and you ought to also.

On the windshield of my car I have three or four police stickers. I believe in supporting the police department. We ought not sit by and allow such things as promoting the killing of police. We need to teach people that God is a God of authority, He puts people in positions of authority, and He requires all under authority to have respect for those who have authority over them.

Hebrews 13:17 commands, "Obey them that have the rule over you, and submit yourselves: for they watch for your souls."

Romans 13:1,2 tells us:

"Let every soul be subject unto the higher powers. For there is no power but of God: the powers that be are ordained of God.

"Whosoever therefore resisteth the power, resisteth the ordinance of God: and they that resist shall receive to themselves damnation."

There are several kinds of authority. There is **governmental** authority; there is **parental** authority; there is the authority of the **teacher**; there is the authority of the **pastor**. Like it or not, the pastor is the head of the church. There was a time when people had respect for pastors, but that day has just about gone. Children have heard their parents criticize their pastor, talk about how much money he makes, the kind of car he drives, and the kind of clothes he wears until they have no more respect for the authority of the man of God. How tragic! That breaks down everything. You see, rebellion against authority **inside** the home is a foretaste of rebellion against authority **outside** the home. Teach them to respect authority.

DON'T WAIT UNTIL
IT IS TOO LATE

Parents should perform their God-given responsibilities before it is too late to be effective.

Don't wait until your children are gone and the only thing you can do is pray **for them**. Do what you need to do while you have them with you and while you can pray **with them**.

To me, one of the most beautiful scenes is to see parents bringing their little children to an altar of prayer. They are praying **with them,** and they will know how to pray **for them** when they are gone.

Bring them to church now. Make up your mind whether your children will go forth from your home as sinners, rebels and agents of vice to serve sin and Satan, or whether they will go as dedicated, consecrated Christians to serve God and man. It is up to you. I appeal to you in the name of Jesus Christ to make the altar a familiar kneeling ground. Ask God to raise up a generation of stalwart soldiers of the cross. Ask God to help you to train that vast army that is growing up so that they will be profitable Christian citizens in the tomorrows. Our destiny depends on it.

Do you want to revolutionize your home and your family? Then put these seven principles into practice, and on the authority of God's Word I assure you that they will revolutionize your home.

ESTABLISHING BIBLICAL STANDARDS FOR EVERY CHRISTIAN HOME

"I beseech you therefore, brethren, by the mercies of God, that ye present your bodies a living sacrifice, holy, acceptable unto God, which is your reasonable service.

"And be not conformed to this world: but be ye transformed by the renewing of your mind, that ye may prove what is that good, and acceptable, and perfect, will of God."—Rom. 12:1,2.

If we are willing to trust God with our souls, we ought to be willing to trust Him with our bodies, because our bodies are the temples of the Holy Spirit. There may come a time when God will want us to die for Jesus Christ, but I am speaking of the present. I don't believe that today God wants us to die for His cause, but I know He does want us to live for Him, to offer our bodies "a living sacrifice, holy, acceptable…."

What has happened to the doctrine of holiness and holy living? "I beseech you therefore, brethren, by the mercies of God, that ye present your bodies a living sacrifice, holy, acceptable unto God, which is your reasonable service." God does not demand of His people anything unreasonable. If He gives us seven days, it is certainly not unreasonable for Him to ask for one day. If God gives us a hundred percent of all we earn and all we have, He is certainly not unreasonable in asking for ten percent. If God gives us life, breath, intelligence, mental faculties, energy, strength and ability, He is certainly not unreasonable in demanding that we give Him all of the things that He outlines within His Book.

Look at verse 2: "And be not conformed to this world,"

to this world system in which we live. Paul says in II Corinthians 6:17,18:

"Wherefore come out from among them, and be ye separate, saith the Lord, and touch not the unclean thing; and I will receive you,

"And will be a Father unto you, and ye shall be my sons and daughters, saith the Lord Almighty."

When Paul commands, "And be not conformed to this world," he is saying not to allow this world to squeeze you into its mold, not to adopt the lifestyle of this world as your lifestyle, not to look like the world, act like the world, talk like the world, think like the world, nor react like the world; but be transformed—taken over into something that is altogether different.

> **Put your body, soul and mind at God's disposal.**

Then Paul says, "...be ye transformed by the renewing of your mind." Paul has addressed the body; now he is addressing the mind. How many hundreds of people have said to me, "Pastor, what is God's will for my life?" or, "How can I discern what God's will is for my life?" Paul says if you want to know what God's will is for your life, put your body on the altar, present it to God, be transformed by the renewing of your mind in order that you might prove (understand, discover, determine, discern) what God's will is for your life. It comes when you put your body, soul and mind at God's disposal.

We are living in a day when anything goes. These are perilous times. If you want an up-to-date account of what is happening in America, all you have to do is turn to II Timothy, chapter 3, where Paul speaks of days of difficulty, degradation, disparity, despondency, sin and greed; when men will be lovers of pleasure more than lovers of God; when men will be heady, high-minded, traitors, disobedient to parents, without natural affection, and on and on. That is just like today's and tomorrow's headlines.

As never before, Christian families must bind themselves together under the umbrella of Christian love. We must present to this sin-sick, sin-cursed, Hell-bound world a united front for Jesus Christ. We must put forth godliness, sobriety, truth, honor, integrity and morality. We must give the world an example of righteousness. The world demands and the world deserves to see something different in you and me. Be not conformed to the world; come out from among the world. Be different. Be dedicated.

It is strange that so many people want to be like everybody else. If one little group dresses one way, we want to dress that way. If one little group does something, we want to do the same. If one little group is involved in this, we want to be involved in it too. Be different! Set apart yourself. Separate yourself. Sanctify yourself, if you please. *Sanctified* means "set apart for a particular purpose."

We have no message but His message, no truth but His truth, no challenge but His challenge, no life but His life, no honor but His honor. We have no sacrifice but His blood, no salvation but His salvation. In fact, without Him we are zero with the rim erased.

THE NECESSITY OF ESTABLISHING BIBLICAL STANDARDS IN THE HOME

Proverbs 29:15 says, "The rod and reproof give wisdom." Correction and discipline bring wisdom into the hearts and minds of children. This verse goes on, "…but a child left to himself [without any restriction, without any restraint, without any discipline, without any correction, without any standard, without any guideline] bringeth his mother to shame."

Unbridled energy can be explosive and dangerous. A home without standards is like a ship without a compass. It is like an automobile without a steering wheel, like an airplane without a gyroscope. Undeniably, human nature demands to be regulated. We can't leave it to do what it wants to do. There must be walls built around us. There must be standards of righteousness for us. We all need guidelines by which to govern our lives. Life itself requires the principles of government. Why do you suppose God established government in the Scripture? He knew the creature He had created would need government, standards, principles, guidelines—things to show us the way.

Standards of life and living are necessary for three reasons: First, standards help to build **character**. If we allow just anything to come into the church and into the home, we will have no character, and the church will have no character. Without standards and regulations, the family would have no character, nor would the nation.

Second, establishing standards keeps us in line with the **teaching of God's Word**. The Bible is our guideline, our manual, our standard of measure.

Third, establishing biblical principles produces a **Christlikeness** that comes only as a result of godly living.

In Acts, chapter 11, people started looking at those who called themselves disciples. They had seen and heard what Christ was like, and when they saw these people walking like Christ walked, living like Christ lived, talking like Christ talked, they said, "They are Christ-ones—Christians."

Many people are living under a Christian flag, in so-called Christian countries, with so-called Christian ideals, who are not really "Christ-ones." When people in your family, on your job, in your group or in your classroom see your lifestyle, listen to your conversation and watch your reactions, would they accuse you of being like Christ? Standards ensure

Christlikeness, which comes only as a result of godly living. That is the absolute necessity.

DIFFICULTIES INVOLVED IN ESTABLISHING STANDARDS IN THE HOME

One difficulty is overcoming the natural resistance to any form of regulation. While deep inside each of us, human nature demands some kind of regulation, a little something in every one of us says, "Oh no! You are not going to put me in that narrow place. You are not going to make me do this or that." There is the obvious difficulty of overcoming natural resistance to any form of regulation.

Another prevalent difficulty is the confusion caused as a result of parental differences of opinion. One parent says, "We are going to let them do anything they want to do. I didn't get to do what I wanted to do when I was young; I want my children to do anything they want to do, go anywhere they want to go." The other one says, "Oh no, we will not! They will not..." A difference of opinion sets up a conflict in the child's mind: he doesn't know whether to go right or left, listen to Mom or Dad.

Parents, get together on methods and means, doctrines and ideals, principles and regulations and standards in your home. If your children hear you argue and dispute, they are going to wonder, *Who is right? Which is the truth? I love Mother, and I know she wouldn't lie. I love Daddy, and I don't think he would lie either. So, who is right?* They are sitting there somewhere in between.

You parents, put together a united front. If you would argue, get in the closet. Don't let the children hear you discussing whether

> **Parents, put together a united front.**

this is right or wrong; don't make it so they have to wonder which parent is right. If you two will take it to God, He will show you who is right. Follow the principles of the Bible and the leadership of the Holy Spirit.

Christian standards based on biblical principles make a family different from the secular world. Your children ask you, "Why do we do this? My friends don't do it"; or, "My friends do this; why don't we do it? Why do we do this? Why do we have to be different?" Can't you tell them that Christians are a different type people? God wants us to be fruit-bearing Christians, not spiritual nuts; but with God's help, you can agree together and explain to your children, "Here is the reason why we don't do this. This is what God says, this is what the Bible says, and this is what we believe. This is the reason we ought to do it (or ought not to do it)."

In many cases, biblical standards will set your family apart from other families within the "Christian" community. All too many of you are patterning your lives after the accepted norm of the "Christian" community, not realizing or not caring that the "Christian" community is going downhill. What you wouldn't have thought of allowing fifteen or twenty years ago, you embrace, sanction and put your approval on now.

The standard of Christian behavior is not in the "Christian" community but in Christ and the Bible. If ordering your life after Jesus Christ means breaking away from the so-called "Christian" community, then break away without hesitation and without reservation.

Many things are labeled "Christian" that are not Christian. We have put the label on a thing just to sanction it with God's approval, but that won't work. You see, if it is wrong, it is wrong even if the "Christian" community as a whole says, "We believe it is right." It is wrong if it is not in agreement with the Word of God and its standards and principles.

We have no other standard; we have no other Book. No psychology book or child-training book matches the Bible. Don't forsake the instructions of God for the instructions of man. The Holy Spirit will help you to interpret right out of the Scriptures what is needed.

Young people, don't think because Mother and Daddy are trying to get you back to the standards of God's Word that they are outdated and old-fashioned. The Bible is newer than any book that will be printed next week, next month or next year. It still has the same basic truth that it has always had. If it was right three thousand years ago, it is right now! It doesn't matter how the "Christian" community labels it or describes it or defines it or delineates it; if it is not in line with the Bible, it is wrong!

DECISIVE ACTION MUST BE TAKEN IN ESTABLISHING STANDARDS IN THE HOME

Parents, define the objectives that you wish to accomplish in establishing standards. In other words, ask yourself, "What are we trying to accomplish by adopting and establishing biblical standards in our home? What objectives are we after?"

Here are some objectives:

1. **Instill respect for authority.** Ask any expert who has done any study, anybody who has the vision to see what is happening in our world, and that one will tell you that disrespect for authority is the reason for the breakdown in the world about us. Establishing standards gives respect for authority.

2. **Definite objectives help in selecting friendships.** You had best be selective in choosing your friends. You say, "But I

want to go where they go, do what they do; that way, I will be able to win them to Christ." Don't bank on it! Even a casual friend may become a steadfast buddy tomorrow; then you will have a stronger decision to make when you have to break away from that friend because your selection proved wrong.

3. **Definite objectives help in dating.** Don't date any person you would not choose for a mate. Five years from now, her beauty won't matter that much. Ten years from now, it won't matter at all. Be careful when you choose a **date**, because one day that person may become your **mate**. Be careful when you are choosing friends; biblical standards will help you choose the right kind.

4. **Established standards help you with the acceptance of responsibility.** The Bible demands responsibility. We are not free-loaders or free spirits to do anything we want to do. We have responsibilities. Establishing biblical principles helps us comply with God's Word.

> The Bible demands responsibility.

5. **Use time properly.** You can waste your time away doing nothing.

A few years ago I did an experiment in a class that I was teaching. I had all the students write down a twenty-four-hour schedule. They started at six o'clock in the morning. I had them put down what they did the first fifteen minutes, the second fifteen minutes—right on down, every fifteen minutes, every hour—right around the clock until six o'clock the next morning. The average student had four to six hours that he could not account for in a twenty-four-hour period.

I know we are all pressed for time, but we do what we want to do in the time we have to do it, or we make time to do it. Budget your time, be responsible for your time, and don't spend so much of your time in foolish and unnecessary things.

6. **The importance of work.** If you follow the Bible, you will know something about the work ethic. There is no pride in America's work force anymore. The work ethic is about gone in America. Two things would correct the economy in America: (1) for God's people to start tithing; (2) for every person to put in a full eight hours' work daily on his job.

7. **Sanctity of life.** We learn to revere life, protect life, born and unborn. Biblical standards give us self-respect. They give us Christian examples. They teach us personal holiness.

Today people are disregarding the truth and embracing every ideology. Vote for people who are right with God, no matter what party they belong to. Your great-grandmother's aunt and uncle's voting for so-and-so or such-and-such a party doesn't mean you ought to. Get involved in the political system. We have too long turned it over to the liberals, politically and religiously. We had better get involved in the political process and see to it that on the grass-roots level we put people in office who honor God's Word, who believe in putting the Bible and prayer back into school, and who will outlaw abortion and all those other things contrary to the Bible.

Without biblical standards, we will let anything and everything come in.

Parents, remember this: **Respect for your rules and regulations comes only after acceptance of your relationship.** If you don't have the right relationship with your children, you are barking up the wrong tree; you are going down a dead-end street; you are wasting your time. Your children aren't going to listen to your rules unless they believe in your relationship. Children accept parental rules because they accept parental relationships. On the other hand, children reject parental rules because they reject the relationship.

Do you know what the key is? Having an IQ of one hundred forty? Oh no. Reading all the books on how to rear children? No, no, no! Then what is the key? Just four little letters—*l-o-v-e*. Season all of your rules, all of your discipline, all of your regulations, all of your standards with **love**.

When a child is loved, he **acts**. When he is not loved, he **reacts**. He knows when love is genuine. You say, "Well, I just love my children so much that I couldn't whip them." Spare the rod, and spoil the child. "He that loveth him [his son] chasteneth him betimes." I am talking about loving **discipline**, taking the child on your lap and telling him that you love him but must whip him while loving him. But don't scare him to death by screaming at him. Don't brutalize him. Don't beat him. Don't shame him to death either. Be loving, kind and understanding. Parental love is a much greater weapon than a razor strap. Be certain to season it all with love. Be certain to explain and help your children to understand by showing them where discipline is taught in the Bible. Show them why these standards are important and why they must comply with them.

> **Live according to the standard you set for your children.**

Now this you don't want to miss: **Be consistent**. Live according to the standard you set for your children—no double standards. If you smoke, there is no need to tell your children not to smoke. If you drink, there is no need to tell your children not to drink. If you are engaged in questionable activities, there is no need to tell your children not to follow you. If you frequent questionable places of entertainment, there is no need to tell your children to frequent only good places. If you dress immodestly, there is no need to tell your children to dress modestly. Be consistent. Children are not looking for **perfection** in you, but they are looking for and expect and deserve **consistency**. Be positive in enforcing your standards. Do everything according to God's will and God's way, not your will nor your way.

When we try to bring ourselves into the twentieth century mode of behavior in our homes and churches, we disregard the moral absolutes and righteous laws of God. The two don't go together. "And be not conformed to this world." Rebellion is wrong. Rioting is wrong. Civil disobedience is wrong. Sex orgies are wrong. Compliance to world standards is wrong. Beer is wrong. Drugs are wrong. As the laws of science are invariable and unchangeable, so are the laws of God.

In determining the rightness or wrongness of our conduct, there are six questions we ought to ask:

1. **Does it glorify God?** A good verse here is I Corinthians 10:31: "Whether therefore ye eat, or drink, or whatsoever ye do, do all to the glory of God."

2. **Does it give the appearance of evil?** I didn't ask if it was evil, but, does it give the **appearance** of evil? In I Thessalonians 5:22 Paul says, "Abstain from all appearance of evil."

3. **Does it entangle my life in the affairs of the world?** Let II Timothy 2:4 answer: "No man that warreth entangleth himself with the affairs of this life; that he may please him who hath chosen him to be a soldier."

4. **Does it hinder other people?** Even if I don't think it is wrong, does it hinder somebody else who might think it is wrong? Would it be a stumbling block to others? Listen to what Paul says in I Corinthians 8:9: "But take heed lest by any means this liberty of yours become a stumblingblock to them that are weak." Remember the question came up, "Should we eat the meat that is offered to idols?" Some said "yes" and some said "no," and Paul said, "Wherefore, if meat make my brother to offend, I will eat no flesh while the world standeth." It may not be wrong for you to do, but if it is going to offend somebody else, it is wrong.

5. **Does it defile my body, my spirit or my mind?** Read I Corinthians 6:19, 20:

"What? know ye not that your body is the temple of the Holy Ghost which is in you, which ye have of God, and ye are not your own?

"For ye are bought with a price: therefore glorify God in your body, and in your spirit, which are God's."

6. **Will it stand at the judgment seat of Christ?** Read II Corinthians 5:10: "For we must all appear before the judgment seat of Christ; that every one may receive the things done in his body, according to that he hath done, whether it be good or bad."

We are living in an hour when we must say, "We are Christians. We are 'Christ-ones.' This is our standard of righteousness, and it is based entirely, completely, totally upon the Bible."

We are "Christ-ones."

ROLE AND RESPONSIBILITY OF PARENTS REGARDING DISCIPLINE

"Train up a child in the way he should go: and when he is old, he will not depart from it."—Prov. 22:6.

There is something about planting the seed of truth, the Word of God and principles of discipline in the hearts and lives of little ones that lasts all their lives. They may *stray* away, but they will not *stay* away.

God Himself ordained the family and structured the family according to the counsel of His own divine wisdom. He ordained parenthood, and He ordained childhood. God instructed Adam and Eve, our first parents, in the Garden of Eden, "Be fruitful, and multiply, and replenish the earth" (Gen. 1:28). That is God's method of reproduction. God governs every aspect and every facet of parenthood.

To new parents who have just had your first baby, parenthood brings not only joy, happiness and privileges, but duties, cares and responsibilities. To you who have just birthed your first baby, your life, your home, your schedule will never be the same. You will sleep less than you ever have in your life. What a joy it is to get up at three o'clock in the morning! While God has brought you joy and happiness through that little one, He has added indescribable responsibilities.

God's plan is workable, equitable and acceptable. My wife and I have never been blessed with children, so you might ask, "Should one who doesn't have children try to tell us how to rear ours?" That is like saying, if a fellow hasn't ever owned a cow, ought he sell milk?

God Himself defines and delineates the role of parents

and what the response of children should be in matters of discipline. He leaves nothing to chance. A divine prescription is written in the Bible. It covers every phase, every aspect and every facet of family relationships. If we study the Word of God as we should, we will come to the conclusion that God tells fathers how to be fathers, mothers how to be mothers, children how to be children, husbands how to be husbands, wives how to be wives, and families how to be families.

I must issue a warning with a stern reminder: There are boundaries in God's plan, prescription and program beyond which we must not go. If we do, we will suffer the consequences. When a family stays within the framework of God's prescribed method of discipline, the proper results can be expected. But when a family steps beyond the boundaries of biblical procedures, plans and prescriptions, that family writes its own prescription for misery, heartache and sorrow.

> **When you delay obedience, it becomes disobedience.**

Parents can disobey too, so I want to discuss your disobedience. When God lays out in His Word how parents are to bring up their children in the fear and admonition and nurture of the Lord and they fail to do that, then they are flagrantly in disobedience. Devastation, destruction and death follow deliberate disobedience, and delayed obedience is tantamount to disobedience. You say, "I am going to, aiming to, one of these days, after we have our second baby." When you delay **obedience**, it becomes **disobedience**.

This chapter is designed to show parents your divinely ordained participation in and execution of child discipline. This subject is of utmost importance when we see what is taking place in our nation today. Surely if our young people had been brought up in the fear and admonition of the Lord, they wouldn't be looting and shooting and killing today. I rather doubt that our schoolteachers would fear for their lives if the children had been brought up in the fear and admonition and nurture of the Lord.

Parents, not until you have done your best with your children can you satisfy God. You have a divinely ordained responsibility to discipline, to train, to bring them up in the nurture of the Lord. So be sure that you do more than bring them to Sunday school or church.

SCRIPTURAL INSTRUCTIONS ON HOW TO PRODUCE DISCIPLINED CHILDREN

On the **regularity of discipline** Proverbs 13:24 reads: "He that spareth his rod hateth his son: but he that loveth him chasteneth him betimes." That word *betimes* means "often," as often as needed. You parents need wisdom, and the best place to get it is out of the book of Proverbs, God's wisdom book. I urge you to read one chapter in Proverbs every day, regardless of any other Bible reading you do. It teaches parents about the regularity of discipline.

The Bible instructs parents to begin discipline at an early age. Notice that the word in the text is *child.* God is talking about little ones. "As the twig is bent, so the tree grows."

> **Begin discipline at an early age.**

A group of parents were trying to decide at what age children should be disciplined. Someone said, "I think it ought to begin at age three." Another said, "I think it shouldn't begin until age six." One dear, old, wise woman in that crowd stood up and said, "I think it ought to begin twenty-five years before the child is born."

Young people, don't forget that one day you too will be a parent. I remind you of something else: When you stand up and point a finger in the face of a parent and call him/her "the old man" or "the old lady," remember that somebody will call you the same thing one of these days. When you show disrespect and disregard for rules, regulations and authority, it will be thrown right back at you. The Bible says, "For whatsoever a man soweth, that shall he also reap." When you go on a rage against your parents, remember this: You will have children one day who will throw it right in your face, and you will deserve it.

Young people, begin now asking God for wisdom in disciplining your children. Early childhood training is of utmost importance. The former director of the F.B.I., J. Edgar Hoover, said, "The cure for crime is not found in the electric chair but in the high chair." Start disciplining your own life before your children are born. If you do not correct them in the playpen, you might find yourself visiting them in the state pen.

> Our problem is we have substituted "Spocking" for spanking.

Proverbs 23 says you are to use corporal punishment: "Withhold not correction from the child: for if thou beatest him with the rod, he shall not die." How many of you ever hollered and screamed and held your breath? Let them hold their breath for a little while; they will catch it back. "Thou shalt beat him with the rod, and shalt deliver his soul from hell" [from destruction].

We have substituted the psychology book for the razor strap. I am not suggesting that you beat your child. Shame on you if you do such a thing! Someone has said, "Some kids are like a ketchup bottle: you have to slap them on the bottom before you can get them moving." He was wise who said, "When children get on the wrong track, it is time to use the switch." Almost everything in the modern home is run by the switch, except the children. And when you parents relegate your authority to them, you are in deep trouble, not just for a day but for all the days of your life.

Put down the psychology book and pick up the switch. Spanking is proof of your love for your child. You may say, "Well, I love him too much to spank him." No, you don't love him at all if you don't discipline him. Proverbs 22:15 reminds us, "Foolishness is bound in the heart of a child; but the rod of correction shall drive it far from him." Sometimes you have to **bend** a child over to **straighten** him out. Someone has said, "More board meetings in the **woodshed** would mean fewer cases in the **courtroom**." You have turned the training of your children over to the Sunday school and the public school and the private school. That won't work. The church can see that you have what you need to do it, but the church can't do it. Don't go around blaming the pastor and the church and God if your children don't turn out right. It surely isn't God's fault, and I rather doubt that it is the fault of the church.

Let me caution you: Wisdom and discretion must govern the measure and degree of corporal punishment. You must differentiate between punishment and discipline. I won't say anything more important than what I am going to say here: **Discipline is the process by which you build a strong and loving relationship with your children, and it is based on mutual respect for each other.** On the other hand, **punishment is payment for an infraction of rules.** Now follow this logic: The stronger the relationship and the greater the respect, the fewer will be the times when punishment has to be executed. What am I saying? You build a good relationship, a mutual understanding, a mutual respect one for the other; then you won't find as many times that you will have to execute punishment.

Warning: Don't shout at your children! They are not deaf. Sometimes in a shopping mall or a supermarket I want to grab some parents and tell them a thing or two. I am amazed when I see the way some of them treat their children. They jerk them up by the arm or by the hair and scream at them. Someone has said, "Don't shout unless the house is on fire."

The Bible instructs you **never to allow a child to be the judge in matters of discipline**. To ask a child, "Do you want a whipping?" is a foolish question. Nobody wants a whipping; or, "Don't you think I ought to discipline you?" Children demand a voice of authority.

One Sunday night a little boy out in the lobby said to my wife, "I'm not going into church." My wife said, "Yes, you are going into church." He said, "Okay." All he needed was somebody with authority.

Children demand it, expect it and need it. Don't ask, "Don't you think you ought to eat this?" Wise up! Don't leave these questions to the children to answer. Proverbs 29:15 and 17 says:

"The rod and reproof give wisdom: but a child left to himself bringeth his mother to shame....

"Correct thy son, and he shall give thee rest; yea, he shall give delight unto thy soul."

Failure to correct the child will bring nothing but unrest. It will bring heartache and misery.

Some of you are now pulling out your hair and wringing your hands because you allow your children to do anything they want to do, anytime they want to do it, anywhere they want to do it. If they want to kick the furniture, you let them kick the furniture. If they want to slap another kid, you let them slap another kid. That is why you are growing old too soon.

How to Raise a Crook

1. Begin from infancy to give the child every-thing he wants. This way he will grow up to believe that the world owes him a living.

2. When he picks up bad words, laugh at him. It will encourage him to pick up "cuter" phrases that will blow the top off your head later on.

3. Never give him any spiritual training. Wait until he is twenty-one, then let him decide for himself.

4. Avoid the use of the word *wrong*. It may develop a guilt complex. This will condition him to believe later, when he is arrested for stealing a car, that society is against him and he is being persecuted.

5. Pick up anything he leaves lying around—books, shoes, clothing, etc. Do everything for him so he will be experienced in throwing the responsibility onto others.

6. Let him read any printed matter he can get his hands on. Be careful the silverware and drinking glasses are sterilized but let his mind feed on garbage.

7. Quarrel frequently in the presence of the children, then they won't be too shocked when the home is broken up.

8. Give the child all the spending money he wants. Never let him earn his own. Why should he have things as tough as you had them?

9. Satisfy his every craving for food, drink and comfort. See that every desire is gratified. Denial may lead to harmful frustrations.

10. Take his part against the neighbors, teachers

and policemen. They are all prejudiced against your child.

11. When he gets into real trouble, apologize for yourselves by saying, "I never could do anything with him."

12. Prepare for a life of grief—you will have it.

Here is a strange phenomenon in the American culture: We fence up our pets and turn our children loose.

How to Train a Child for Real Trouble

Once there was a little boy. When he was three weeks old his parents turned him over to a baby-sitter.

When he was two years old, they dressed him up like a cowboy and gave him a gun.

When he was three, everybody said, "Ain't he cute!" as he went about lisping a beer commercial.

When he was six, his father occasionally dropped him off at Sunday school on his own way to the golf course.

When he was eight, his parents bought him a BB gun and taught him to shoot birds. He learned to shoot windshields by himself.

When he was ten, he spent his afternoons squatting at the drugstore newsstand reading comic books. His mother wasn't at home, and his father was very busy.

When he was thirteen, he told his parents that other boys stayed out as late as they wanted to, so they said he could too. It was easier that way.

When he was fifteen, the police called his home one midnight. "We have your boy here at the station. He's in trouble."

"In trouble?" screamed the father. "It can't be *my* boy!"

If you train them for trouble, you will get trouble. Permissiveness is **poisonous,** but discipline is **profitable.** The Apostle Paul in Hebrews 12:9–11 compared it to God's discipline of us:

> Permissiveness is poisonous, but discipline is profitable.

"*Furthermore we have had fathers of our flesh which corrected us, and we gave them reverence* [If parents will scripturally chasten their children, the children will show their parents reverence]: *shall we not much rather be in subjection unto the Father of spirits, and live?*

"*For they verily for a few days chastened us after their own pleasure; but he for our profit, that we might be partakers of his holiness.*

"*Now no chastening for the present seemeth to be joyous....*"

Remember when Daddy used to say, "Son, I am doing this for your own good"?

The last old-fashioned whipping I got was when I was a senior in high school. I talked back to a man who came to our door to sell something, and my mother overheard it. I didn't know my mother overheard what I said to that guy. I thought I was somebody! "We don't need your products. What are you doing on our doorstep?" When Daddy got home, Mother said, "Rob, I want to tell you something about your little fair-haired boy, your soon-to-be high school graduate." Then she told him what I had said.

Daddy took me to the bedroom, got his belt and whipped me—a senior in high school!

It is important that you discipline and punish because you love and because it is profitable. "Now no chastening for the present seemeth to be joyous, but grievous: nevertheless afterward it yieldeth the peaceable fruit of righteousness unto them which are exercised thereby." It produces righteousness in those upon whom it is inflicted.

SUGGESTED PRINCIPLES ON HOW TO DEVELOP CHARACTER IN CHILDREN

Surely all of you want your children to grow up with character, so here are seven basic principles to follow:

1. Keep a close vigil on their actions, acquaintances and attitudes. That is, watch closely **what** they do, with **whom** they do it, and their **attitude** toward it.

2. Exercise your divinely prescribed role of leadership. You are the leader; exercise your divinely ordained role of leadership.

3. Lead them early in their search for God. Don't let them grow up and choose the religion they want, the church they want to attend, and just anything they want to do. A good parent doesn't let young children choose what they are going to eat, or the clothes they will wear, or the school they will attend. Don't say, "I will let them choose God **if** they want to, **when** they want to." Begin **early** in their lives.

4. Keep them busy in worthwhile family-related projects. If you send them out to the YMCA or the YWCA or the day camp, they will think home is not important. Get some family-related projects that will keep them busy at home.

5. Assign definite responsibilities and **see that they are carried out**. If you do everything for them instead of putting them in a mode of independence, you do them an injustice. If you assign them a job which they don't want to do and you go right ahead and do it, what are you doing? Molding them

in such a way that when they get out in the world, they won't know how to face responsibility. They won't know how to get a job, how to get along with people, how to take any responsibility whatsoever. Give them responsibility now, and see that it is carried out.

6. Provide a **challenge**, a storehouse of new ideas.

7. Make home the **focal point** and **central attraction**. Let them know that their home is important. Make it attractive for them, so they will be attached to the home, will love the home and what goes on there. Provide some things outside, but don't let anything take the central focal point that the home should have.

There is no place like home. It is sad, but some children don't want to go home after school because they know they are going to face bickering parents or they themselves will be screamed at. What happens in cases like that? They start staying out a bit later in the afternoon. They are supposed to be home at 4:00; they will start staying away until 4:15. If this type of thing continues, they will stay away until about 4:30. They don't want to go home until they have to. Then they will stay away until 5:00. Before long, they won't even come home for supper because their house is a dreaded place, an armed camp.

Then they start going to somebody else's house; the same thing is happening there. So two or three get together and say, "Why don't we go down to the park?" Then after awhile they get awfully bored at the park. There is just so much you can do there. Then they go down to the Seven-Eleven. They haven't had any supper; so when the clerk turns his head, they reach for and get a candy bar. After all, it is just fifty cents. After awhile, not being satisfied with just a candy bar, they get a bag of cookies.

Then later they say, "We got by with stealing the candy

bar and the bag of cookies, so why don't we steal a car?" And they steal a car.

Later they say, "We don't have any money, and Mother and Daddy aren't going to give us any, so why don't we rob a store?" So they rob a store.

You know where it started? They hated to go home because they knew Mother and Daddy were going to be quarreling or cross and irritable.

I beg you, make your home the focal point and central attraction for your children.

SENSIBLE ADMONITIONS ON HOW TO KEEP CHILDREN ON YOUR TEAM

Consider yourself a manager with team members. I have four admonitions for you to consider:

1. Your **thoughts** toward your children must be proper. Think of them as gifts from God, for after all, that is what they are. "Lo, children are an heritage of the LORD: and the fruit of the womb is his reward" (Ps. 127:3).

2. Your **treatment** of them must be proper. Lovingly accept your children by showing a genuine interest in their interests. If you keep saying to that little fellow or to that precious girl, "I don't have time to check your schoolwork; I don't have time to look at that project; I have too many things to do," he or she is are going to start turning to somebody else, and that somebody else is going to gain his/her affection and respect. Don't lose your children because you are too busy to show interest in what they are interested in. Listening, experiencing, feeling, identifying, sharing—all are vitally important!

3. Your **teaching** of them must be proper. Teach them

the principles of right and wrong as outlined in the Bible. Don't depend on psychology books. Some are good, but the Bible is the greatest Book of mental, spiritual and emotional therapy that has ever been written.

You may say, "Well, I just can't understand the Bible." Chances are, you haven't given yourself a chance to understand it because you are too busy watching television, or reading magazines, or trotting to the neighbor's house, or going somewhere else. You don't take time to sit down with your children and read them the Word of God. That is what's wrong in America. Don't blame it on the church nor the school. Sit down with the Word of God and share it with them.

There were nine children in our family. Daddy was one of the busiest of preachers. He had a radio broadcast and, after sixty years, that broadcast is still going on every day. He traveled. It was nothing for him to drive 150 miles on a Sunday afternoon between morning and evening services to preach to a group of people without a pastor, then drive back to his pastorate to preach that night. He conducted revival meetings and Bible conferences all over Virginia and North Carolina. But I can't remember one day when my daddy didn't read a few verses of Scripture and have prayer with his family. When he was out of town, Mother took his place.

Don't tell me that you are too busy. You would take time if you really knew the dimension and the depth and the necessity of it. Take time to be holy. Take time to read the Word of God to your children. Don't expect the preacher to feed you all of it; get some of it for yourself.

> **Take time to read the Word of God to your children.**

J. Frank Norris, at the turn of the century, established a Bible institute so young men with no college training could come from behind the plow, out of the factories and into a classroom to learn the Word of God and how to win souls and how to build churches. That is still being talked about today.

All over America there are independent, fundamental Baptist churches and Baptist preachers because somebody thought it important to train others. If Jesus tarries, twenty-five or fifty years from now, young men will be standing behind pulpits because some other preachers trained God-called men to preach and to build churches.

Do you get the point? Do you see what I am saying? The same thing can be applied to your home. What you are doing for your children **today** will be talked about twenty-five years from now, when those disciplined and trained young people with character go out and light a light for Jesus in a dark and dismal world. So don't despair. When you teach them the principles of right and wrong, it will be remembered and seen in those lives for years to come.

4. Your **testimony** before them must be proper. This is most important because what we do speaks much louder than what we say. If Mother and Daddy eat onions and garlic, you shouldn't expect your children to smell like roses. Let them see a genuine Christlikeness in your life. If the dye has been in the wool, it is hard to get it out of the cloth. The best way to keep your children on your team is to assure them that you are on their team.

Here are some pertinent questions that every parent ought to ask and answer regarding his children:

- Do I manifest a genuine love and sincere concern for them?
- Do I sense their spiritual, social and psychological needs?
- Do I provide a spiritual atmosphere in which they can grow up?

- Do I project a good image as I strive to give them a godly role model?

- Do I maintain a positive attitude toward their fears, failures and frustrations?

- Do I provoke them to anger in matters that are unimportant and irrelevant?

- Do I do my best to cultivate with my children a loving, lasting relationship built on mutual respect?

Your children are the only earthly possessions that you can take with you to Heaven.

THE RESPONSE OF CHILDREN TO PARENTAL AUTHORITY

God speaks to all areas of our lives: things we need, things we depend upon, things we must have to get through life. One of those things has to do with **discipline** and **obedience** of children. Paul addresses that from the standpoint of both children and parents:

"Children, obey your parents in the Lord: for this is right.

"Honour thy father and mother; which is the first commandment with promise;

"That it may be well with thee, and thou mayest live long on the earth.

"And, ye fathers, provoke not your children to wrath: but bring them up in the nurture and admonition of the Lord."—Eph. 6:1–4.

In the last chapter we established some basic principles for parents. Let me mention by way of review just three of them. First, you have a God-given role of leadership, and this leadership must not be relegated to anybody else. Second, you have a divinely prescribed pattern of discipline. You cannot improve on God's principles and God's precepts for bringing your children up in the fear and admonition of the Lord. Third, you are accountable to God for the proper upbringing of your children. God is not going to hold the state responsible, nor the church, nor the school system. The responsibility and the accountability are squarely on your shoulders.

A local television station used to put on the screen at night: "It is ten o'clock; do you know where your children are?" Let me say this on behalf of your children: It is also important for them to know where Mother and Daddy are. Let me give you this warning from Proverbs 29:15: "A child left to himself bringeth his mother to shame." Children left unattended, unsupervised, uncared-for and undisciplined will become uncontrollable, unmanageable and unteachable.

How should they respond to your authority?

OBEDIENCE AND HONOR

Children are instructed in God's Word to render obedience and honor to their parents. This is what the Bible says. We are not guessing nor taking this from somebody's book on child training.

When is a child a child? As long as he gets from his parents his protection, his sustenance, his housing, his clothing, his food and all other things necessary for living. "Children, **obey** your parents." Let me expand a bit on that.

> Honor is due for a lifetime.

What about this business of **honoring**? I am over sixty, but if my mother and daddy were living, I would still honor their wishes to the best of my ability. We are not excused from honoring our parents when we get to be twenty-one. Honor is due for a lifetime. The text spells it out very clearly: "Children, obey your parents." Colossians 3:20 also says, "Children, obey your parents in all things: for this is well pleasing unto the Lord."

Let's consider that word *obedience.* **Obedience** is **right**, obedience is **righteous**, obedience is the **just** and **honorable** thing to do. **Obedience** brings **glory** to God. **Obedience** brings **good** to the child, brings **harmony** to the home and is well pleasing to the Lord. **Obedience** results in a **happy** and **productive** life. Obeying your parents assures that life will be good to you.

Not only that, obedience brings assurance of long life. Many things that some of you are involved in may be dangerous. Obedience will keep you from the dangers and evils that tend to shorten your life.

For example, your parents tell you not to drink. But you go out and get inebriated; you drive down the highway and kill yourself and somebody else. You cut your life short because you didn't obey your parents. You involved yourself in something dangerous and evil that tends to shorten one's life.

The word *obey* means "to hearken to a command and continuously submit to it." In other words, *obey* is continuous present tense, and it means "keep on obeying." We could well read Ephesians 6:1, 'Children, keep on obeying your parents,' and do no injustice to the Scripture. It is the same verb tense that Jesus used when He said in Matthew 7:7, "Ask, and it shall be given you; seek, and ye shall find; knock, and it shall be opened unto you." What He really said was, 'Keep on asking, keep on knocking, keep on seeking.' That is the same tense for the word *obey*. Keep on obeying your parents; for this is right, this is righteous, this is just.

Let's consider the word *honor*. It means "to manifest respect and reverence for." Honoring your mother and your father means that you abide by their wishes, respect their judgment and trust their love.

Even if they are a hundred and you are seventy-five, you still are to honor your parents. To honor your mother and father is not just for young children and teens; it is for everybody. If you are thirty-five and you don't honor your parents, shame on you! You ought to ask God's forgiveness. After all, the ones who gave you life are deserving of your respect and love.

Children ought not obey parents just because they are scared to death of them. You ought not structure your disciplinary actions so children are scared of you. They should obey, not from fear, not from intimidation, not from threat, but from love and admiration. Don't blame it all on the kids if they can't find it in their hearts to love and admire you. Examine your own heart and see if there is some shortcoming in your life that hinders.

Children, the Scripture commands you to obey your parents in **all** things.

- Be submissive even when you think they are wrong or when you disagree with their decision.
- Be submissive when you think you should get the car but they think otherwise.
- Be submissive when they say "no" to some form of entertainment that you want to involve yourself in.
- Be submissive when they say "no" to someone you want to date.

Most parents can read character. When they say "no" to certain friends, to certain companions, to certain relationships, honor their wisdom. Biblical admonitions that regulate obedience are for you, not just for somebody else in another culture or somebody who lived two thousand years ago. God's Word is crystal clear in matters of children's responding to parental discipline:

"My son, hear the instruction of thy father, and forsake not the law of thy mother:

"For they shall be an ornament of grace unto thy head, and chains about thy neck.

"My son, if sinners entice thee, consent thou not."—Prov. 1:8–10.

If a group of guys are up to nothing good, and if they are ready to rob a store or do something evil against the law of God and man, don't consent to it, don't follow after them.

"My son, walk not thou in the way with them; refrain thy foot from their path:

"For their feet run to evil, and make haste to shed blood."—Prov. 1:15, 16.

"My son, forget not my law; but let thine heart keep my commandments:

"For length of days, and long life, and peace, shall they add to thee."—Prov. 3:1, 2.

"My son, despise not the chastening of the Lord; neither be weary of his correction:

"For whom the Lord loveth he correcteth; even as a father the son in whom he delighteth."—Prov. 3:11, 12.

"Hear, ye children, the instruction of a father, and attend to know understanding."—Prov. 4:1.

"Hear, O my son, and receive my sayings; and the years of thy life shall be many."—Prov. 4:10.

"Keep thy heart with all diligence; for out of it are the issues of life.

"Put away from thee a froward mouth [Don't be a smart-aleck], *and perverse lips put far from thee."*—Prov. 4:23, 24.

Don't talk ugly or unkindly. Don't make dirty jokes a part of your life. Don't talk back to your parents, nor to the boss, nor to your teacher. Did you ever get popped in the mouth? Some of us deserved it more times than we got it. My daddy used to say, "Son, if I ever again hear you saying those ugly words, I am going to wash your mouth out with Octagon soap." Some of us are still blowing bubbles!

"Let thine eyes look right on, and let thine eyelids look straight before thee.

"Ponder the path of thy feet, and let all thy ways be established."—Prov. 4:25, 26.

"My son, keep my words, and lay up my commandments with thee.

"Keep my commandments, and live; and my law as the apple of thine eye.

"Bind them upon thy fingers, write them upon the table of thine heart."—Prov. 7:1-3.

This is God's Word. I can't improve on it. Dr. Spock can't improve on it. The latest book on psychology and child rearing can't improve on it. This is as old as time, yet as fresh as tomorrow.

"A wise son maketh a glad father: but a foolish son is the heaviness of his mother."—Prov. 10:1.

"A wise son heareth his father's instruction: but a scorner heareth not rebuke."—Prov. 13:1.

"He that wasteth his father, and chaseth away his mother, is a son that causeth shame, and bringeth reproach.

"Cease, my son, to hear the instruction that causeth to err from the words of knowledge."—Prov. 19:26,27.

"Whoso keepeth the law is a wise son: but he that is a companion of riotous men shameth his father."—Prov. 28:7.

Young men and young women, I have given you enough of the Word of God to stabilize your conduct, to guard and govern and guide your life, to give you light, illumination and understanding so that you can start tomorrow a new day, with a new philosophy, a new determination, a new desire, a new dedication to honor your father and your mother. And it shall be well with thee.

Children are taught, commanded and instructed to render obedience and honor to Mother and Father.

CONSEQUENCES OF DISOBEDIENCE

Children are warned of the consequences of disobeying and dishonoring their parents. Children are to show respect to Mom and Dad under all circumstances. Your friends may think your parents a bit old-fashioned and too strict, but you will see the time when you appreciate those who had your best interest at heart and said to you, "No, you can't do that. No, it is not going to happen to you. No, you cannot stay out all night on a date. No, you are not to involve yourself in drugs and alcohol."

Honor, respect, obey, follow through and keep on obeying, even when you don't think your folks know what they are talking about. When you are seventeen, you are a lot smarter than Daddy. But by the time you get to twenty-one, you learn how smart Daddy was and how dumb you were.

"There is a generation that curseth their father, and doth not bless their mother.

"There is a generation that are pure in their own eyes, and yet is not washed from their filthiness.

"There is a generation, O how lofty are their eyes! and their eyelids are lifted up.

"There is a generation, whose teeth are as swords, and their jaw teeth as knives, to devour the poor from off the earth, and the needy from among men."—Prov. 30:11–14.

Please don't miss this. The harmony in many homes is disturbed by two things:

First is the lack of discipline. Parents, harmony breaks down where there is no discipline. In any home where there are not rules and regulations, discipline and training, there is misery. You are writing your own prescription for a miserable household.

Second is the lack of obedience. Children, if you want your home to be a happy place, be submissive and obedient. Honor your father and mother, abide by their wishes, trust their love and believe their judgment.

The society, the culture in which we live, is disintegrating because the homes are disintegrating. Disobedience to parents is a symptom of the total disintegration of a society. Disobedience to parents is listed among the cardinal sins of this age. God, by His Holy Spirit, lists disobedience to parents among the most hideous crimes that men can be guilty of.

"And even as they did not like to retain God in their knowledge, God gave them over to a reprobate mind, to do those things which are not convenient;

"Being filled with all [Listen to this catalogue of sins] *unrighteousness, fornication, wickedness, covetousness, maliciousness; full of envy, murder, debate, deceit, malignity; whisperers,*

"Backbiters, haters of God, despiteful, proud, boasters, inventors of evil things, disobedient to parents,

"Without understanding, covenantbreakers, without natural affection, implacable, unmerciful:

"Who knowing the judgment of God, that they which commit such things are worthy of death, not only do the same, but have pleasure in them that do them."—Rom. 1:28–32.

Do you realize what Paul is saying? All these sins, including disobedience to parents, are worthy of death.

"This know also, that in the last days perilous times shall come.

"For men shall be lovers of their own selves, covetous, boasters, proud, blasphemers, disobedient to parents, unthankful, unholy,

"Without natural affection, trucebreakers, false accusers, incontinent, fierce, despisers of those that are good,

"Traitors, heady, highminded, lovers of pleasures more than lovers of God."—II Tim. 3:1–4.

In both of those passages, Paul is pointing out the cardinal, heinous crimes of our day. In the midst of his list of sins is **children being disobedient to their parents.** That is a part of the disintegration of our society. Disobedience to parents has caused much of the lawlessness, crime and family violence that have disgraced and defamed our nation. Have you ever heard of so much family violence—killing of parents, killing of children, etc.? Somewhere there has been a breakdown in authority. Somewhere we have lost respect for authority. Children who do not obey authority in the **home** are not likely to obey authority in the **school**, in the **church**, in the **government** or in **business.** If they don't obey the rules and regulations of **home,** they are not going to obey the rules and regulations of the **state.** Don't expect them to be **angels** in the classroom when they are **devils** at home right under your eye.

The Bible has an interesting story about young children who do not respect their elders.

Elijah was a prophet of God. It just so happened that he had lost all of his hair. It was a sport in those days to make fun of bald-headed men. We read in II Kings 2:23, 24:

"And he [Elijah] *went up from thence unto Beth-el: and as he was going up by the way, there came forth little children out of the city, and mocked him, and said unto him, Go up, thou bald head; go up, thou bald head.*

"And he turned back, and looked on them, and cursed them in the name of the LORD. And there came forth two she bears out of the wood, and tare forty and two children of them."

Be careful not to disrespect authority. I rather doubt that a bear is going to come out of the woods to get you, but God has more things than bears to execute His judgment.

I can remember—as many of you can—when I was growing up, everyone had respect for a policeman. I was scared to death of one. Any person who had on a uniform brought fear, even a soldier or sailor.

Do you know where disrespect started? In the home. When you don't have authority over your children in the home, they will not respect authority outside the home. They are going to spit at the police, throw rocks at the police, and make fun of the police because they are missing something at home. Don't blame it on the school or the church. Put the blame where it belongs. Parents, even if your kid doesn't like authority, teach him to respect it.

The consequences of disobedience are very severe. What happened to a disobedient son in the Old Testament? We might call him a prodigal—a wayward, rebellious son. Look at Deuteronomy 21:18–20:

> The consequences of disobedience are very severe.

"If a man have a stubborn and rebellious son, which will not obey the voice of his father, or the voice of his mother, and that, when they have chastened him, will not hearken unto them:

"Then shall his father and his mother lay hold on him, and bring him out unto the elders of his city, and unto the gate of his place;

"And they shall say unto the elders of his city, This our son is stubborn and rebellious, he will not obey our voice; he is a glutton, and a drunkard."

Will the men of his city get together and say, "'He had a poor childhood. He was abused when he was just a little baby, so you have to excuse anything that...'"?

I am so tired of laying the blame on something that happened psychologically twenty-five years ago. We can't excuse what is happening and say in every case, "The reason he raped that women was that he was abused when he was a child." I don't believe that! Sin is sin, and it is in the heart. That is why we have to get them under the sound of the

Gospel. That is why every parent ought to sacrifice everything to have every child in church regularly. Let's quit blaming some kind of environmental problem and get to the root of it—S-I-N. Much of the blame lies at the door of parents who let their children **do** what they want to **do** and **go** where they want to **go**!

The child comes home after the teacher has corrected him, and you get mad at the teacher. Wait a minute! About ninety-nine out of a hundred times it is not the teacher's fault, not the principal's fault, not the school's fault, not the Sunday school's fault, not the church's fault. It is **your** fault; it is the **child's** fault. It all started in the home.

Remember, an apple doesn't fall too far from the tree.

In Deuteronomy 21, all the men of the city didn't get together and rationalize and psychoanalyze this little fellow and say, "Well, he just didn't have a chance while growing up." But the Bible says, "And all the men of his city shall stone him with stones, that he die: so shalt thou put evil away from among you; and all Israel shall hear, and fear."

Don't miss this: **If you go after what you do not need, you will end up with what you do not want.** That is a philosophy of life. Sin will take you further than you want to **go**. It will keep you longer than you want to **stay**. It will cost you more than you want to **pay**. This prodigal son of the Old Testament was stoned to death.

The story of the Prodigal Son in the New Testament is in Luke 15. Instead of the father's **stoning** him, he is **seeking** him. Instead of the father's

> **Grace is greater than all our sins!**

killing him, he is **kissing** him. Instead of the father's **rejecting** him, he is **restoring** him. The difference is the **grace of God.** That father in the New Testament, under the Jewish law, could have done to the Prodigal Son what the Old Testament fathers did—execute him. **But grace is greater than**

all our sins! Oh, thank God for His marvelous grace. If we got what we deserved, we would all have awakened in Hell this morning. If we got what we deserved, the lashing of God would be upon us. We would all be stoned but for the grace of God.

Children are instructed to honor and respect, and those instructions must be given by parents. Children must recognize the consequences of disobedience.

PROPER GUIDELINES

Children must be given proper guidelines by their parents. Too many parents are depending on **outside** influences to provide what their children need.

"And these words, which I command thee this day, shall be in thine heart:

"And thou shalt teach them diligently unto thy children, and shalt talk of them when thou sittest in thine house, and when thou walkest by the way, and when thou liest down, and when thou risest up." — Deut. 6:6, 7.

Why don't you unplug that television, gather the family together, and talk about the things of the Lord? Hollywood is not going to help your children be any better. Homosexuality, freedom of love and other things on television are poisonous. Many of you are making the den the classroom and the television the teacher.

A gang bumped a man's car on Interstate 30. When the man stopped, they got out and pumped six bullets into him. Why? They probably saw it done on television and tried to reenact the whole thing.

You say, "Well now, television really doesn't influence people." Whom are you kidding? You are not that stupid! As a grown adult—sixty years, seventy years, eighty years, whatever—you know that television influences your own mind. Every external influence in the world has some bearing on our brains. So we must be careful what we allow to enter our heads through the doors of our eyes. The psalmist said, "I will set no wicked thing before mine eyes." He was saying, "I will not even look at it." Unplug the television, get the family together, and talk about family things.

"And thou shalt bind them for a sign upon thine hand, and they shall be as frontlets between thine eyes.

"And thou shalt write them upon the posts of thy house, and on thy gates."—Deut. 6:8, 9.

This passage says it is important for you to teach children the Word of God. It is the father's duty to give instructions; it is the children's duty to be attentive. As the highways have yellow lines to make for safe travel, so the highway of life must have some yellow lines—rules of the road, if you please:

Do not smoke your first cigarette.

Do not drink your first beer.

Do not take your first dose of drugs.

Let me give you a stern warning: **Little** things become **big** things. I can take sewing thread and bind you where you can't get yourself loose. I can take a number fifty sewing thread and wrap it around your wrist once. You will break it the first time. I will wrap it around two times, and you will break it. Three times and it can be broken. Some of you stronger guys may break the thread after six, seven, eight or nine wraps. But let me put that whole spool of sewing thread around your wrist, and not a man can break it, not one. I am saying, little things become big things.

Nobody ever became a **chain smoker** by smoking a

thousand packages of cigarettes. It all started with one puff.

Nobody ever became an **alcoholic** by drinking ten bottles of whiskey. It all started with one beer.

Nobody ever became a **drug addict** by popping a ton of pills. It all started with one pill.

The old Chinese proverb says:

> Sow a thought; reap a deed.
> Sow a deed; reap a habit.
> Sow a habit; reap a character.
> Sow a character; reap a destiny.

It all starts with something **little**, then it becomes awfully **big**, then you become enslaved and cannot break the habit. God have mercy!

Here are seven **divine directives for dynamic living** for children and young people:

1. **Receive Jesus Christ as your Saviour.** John 1:11, 12 says,

"He came unto his own, and his own received him not.

"But as many as received him, to them gave he power to become the sons of God, even to them that believe on his name."

Have you believed? Have you trusted Jesus Christ?

2. **Keep the lamp of Christian living burning brightly in your life.** Matthew 5:16 says, "Let your light so shine before men, that they may see your good works, and glorify your Father which is in heaven." Young people, let the light of Christ shine. Be juvenile enough to say, "This little light of mine, I'm going to let it shine. This little light of mine, I'm going to let it shine, let it shine, let it shine, let it shine."

3. **Stay within the guidelines of scriptural authority.**

"Now therefore hearken unto me, O ye children: for blessed are they that keep my ways.

104

"Hear instruction, and be wise, and refuse it not.

"Blessed is the man that heareth me, watching daily at my gates, waiting at the posts of my doors."—Prov. 8:32–34.

Keep your lives within the guidelines of the Word of God.

4. Incorporate the very best ideals into your thinking. Remember, "For as he thinketh in his heart, so is he." You are not what you **think** you are, but what you **think**, you **are.** Philippians 4:8 says, "Finally, brethren, whatsoever things are true, whatsoever things are honest, whatsoever things are just, whatsoever things are pure, whatsoever things are lovely, whatsoever things are of good report; if there be any virtue, and if there be any praise, think on these things."

5. Treat parents with the same respect and honor as you would like your children to treat you. Galatians 6:7 says, "Be not deceived; God is not mocked: for whatsoever a man soweth, that shall he also reap."

6. Preserve the biblical principles of honesty, morality and purity. Don't be ashamed that you are still a virgin. Be proud of it. Don't give in to outside influences.

The consequences of disobedience as stated in the Bible are as real in the 1990s as they were in 1492. Young people, keep your virginity. Be pure, be moral, be honest, be upright. If you have failed God in that area, get down on your knees and ask His forgiveness and promise Him you will preserve it from this moment on. His blood will wash you whiter than snow. Listen to I Timothy 5:22: "Neither be partaker of other men's sins: keep thyself pure."

Don't get involved with a gang. If "everybody is doing it," that doesn't make it right. If everybody goes home and strikes a match to his house and sets it on fire and burns his family to death, that doesn't make it right. If everybody goes down to the Southland Life building and jumps off, that doesn't make it right. If all go out and get drunk tonight, that doesn't make it right. If all of your class members on senior prom night get drunk, don't you get drunk. In fact, don't even be at the prom. Because "they" are doing it doesn't make it right. Be virtuous, be honorable, be honest. The last part of verse 22 says, "Keep thyself pure."

7. **Leave footprints behind that will guide those who follow you.** Paul says in Philippians 3:17, "Brethren, be followers together of me, and mark them which walk so as ye have us for an ensample." Be a good example.

There are probably some things you will have to change in order to govern your life by these seven divine directives.

You may have to discard some of the books and magazines you are now reading. Pornographic literature is poisoning the minds of young people all over the world. By the way, do you know what the root for the word *porno* is? It is *harlot*. Put *graphic* on it, which means "to spell out or to write." That reduces you to the level of a harlot when you read pornographic materials. Read the Word of God, read good books.

You may have to choose more carefully the television programs you watch and the movies you see. R-rated, X-rated movies, videos—if you have them, burn them. If you have pornographic literature, burn it. Be careful about the television programs you watch. Parents, know what your children are watching on TV. Know what videos they are bringing home, and be careful about the ones you bring home for them to watch!

You may have to be more selective in the company you keep and the friends you make. A **casual** association can become a **binding** relationship. Be careful with whom you go out, whom you call buddy, whom you call friend, whom you associate with, whom you date. Just a fleeting association may one day become a binding relationship. I admonish you to submit yourself to the authority of God as prescribed in God's Word through the authority of your parents.

The hope of **tomorrow** lies in youth. The world is not going to provide morality. Money can't buy it. Education can't train it. Only God, through godly parents, can provide this instruction.

Children and young people, I say again, submit yourselves to the authority of God through the authority of your parents so that when you get older and on your own, married and bringing little children into the world, you can thank God that you listened to your parents: you will be wanting your children to listen to you.

For children to respond correctly to the training of their parents, they must be:

• Instructed in God's Word to render obedience and honor to parents.

• Warned of the consequences of disobeying and dishonoring parents.

• Given proper guidelines by parents.

TEN COMMANDMENTS FOR TEENAGERS

"Let no man despise thy youth; but be thou an example of the believers, in word, in conversation, in charity, in spirit, in faith, in purity.

"Till I come, give attendance to reading, to exhortation, to doctrine.

"Neglect not the gift that is in thee, which was given thee by prophecy, with the laying on of the hands of the presbytery.

"Meditate upon these things; give thyself wholly to them; that thy profiting may appear to all.

"Take heed unto thyself, and unto the doctrine; continue in them: for in doing this thou shalt both save thyself, and them that hear thee."—I Tim. 4:12–16.

Not only do parents need to set the proper example within the framework of the home, but young people also need to be examples. Look at the words of Paul to young Timothy: 'Let no one despise your youth.' Don't let them say that he is just a youngster or she is just a young girl. "…But be thou an example of the believers, in word, in conversation [lifestyle], in charity, in spirit, in faith, in purity." Paul valued young people so much that he wrote two inspired books to the young man Timothy.

The young people of today are the men and women of tomorrow. We are not going to the honky-tonks, to the dives, to the theaters, and to other such places to choose young people to train to be leaders of tomorrow; we are going to get them right out of our own group. Today's youth are destined to be tomorrow's leaders in the church, in the community, in the nation, and in the world.

Somebody says, "But I know him too well to think he

could ever be a leader anywhere." I wonder if people said that about Churchill, about Roosevelt, about Hitler. These men, good or bad, were once leaders of the world and were one time just youngsters. They were not born full-grown, trained, educated leaders. They came the same way everybody else did. So there is great potential. Teenagers have a **dynamic potential** that must be developed. That is why churches make the investment they do in young people. My text says, 'Look at the potential they have in being the right kind of example.'

We need to understand that teenagers are undergoing a period of **devastating transition** in their lives and must be guided by those who are older and wiser. Look at the scriptural admonition in Proverbs 1:8: "My son, hear the instruction of thy father, and forsake not the law of thy mother."

Teenagers are teachable and must be taught. Proverbs 4:1 advises, "Hear, ye children, the instruction of a father, and attend to know understanding."

Teenagers must be willing to undergo chastening, discipline and correction. Proverbs 3:11 says, "My son, despise not the chastening of the LORD; neither be weary of his correction."

Teenagers should govern their lives by the principles of God's Word. There are many bad principles and forces of evil out there in the world. Evil will be pulling at them and vying for their attention, but teenagers must learn to allow the principles of God's Word to govern their lives. It is thus written in Proverbs 7:1–3:

"My son, keep my words, and lay up my commandments with thee.

"Keep my commandments, and live; and my law as the apple of thine eye.

"Bind them upon thy fingers, write them upon the table of thine heart."

We readily see the potential that teenagers have. There is enough spiritual energy in them to turn the world to Jesus Christ. There is enough spiritual talent, energy and dedication in our youth to turn this nation to God. It doesn't take five thousand young people; God often works through a minority. Look at Gideon and his three hundred against unnumbered thousands.

Let me recommend ten commandments for teenagers:

I. DON'T DRUG OR BOOZE; YOU ARE SURE TO LOSE

I tell you right up front—**boozers** are **losers**. Have you read the statistics lately? Fourteen teenagers die every day in America as a result of drinking drivers. The drug traffic is claiming more lives each day. So, between drugs and alcohol, which is itself a drug, many lives are being snuffed out prematurely and unnecessarily.

Oh, somebody says, "But isn't it all right to take a social drink once in awhile?" Listen! Social drinking leads to disastrous consequences. A social drinker has the same relationship to an **alcoholic** as a pig does to a hog. **Pigs grow up to be hogs.** Hello? You got it? Same relationship. Avoid the first drink. Nobody ever became an alcoholic by sitting down and consuming five barrels of whiskey: it all started with one sip. One drink can be disastrous. The consequences are many, and the price is too high to pay.

> Social drinking leads to disastrous consequences.

Drugs and alcohol will **desecrate** your body. Every time a person takes one swallow of alcohol, it deteriorates a number of the cells in his/her brain; and God knows that most of us cannot stand too much deterioration in that particular area!

It **desecrates** your body.
It **decimates** your mind.
It **dims** your vision.
It **destroys** your spirit.
It will ultimately **damn** your soul.

We ought to admit that booze does make a man very colorful. It gives him a red nose, a white liver, a yellow streak and a blue outlook. Here is a scriptural admonition: "Wine is a mocker, strong drink is raging: and whosoever is deceived thereby is not wise" (Prov. 20:1).

Some think that with one drink in them they are smarter than anybody else. But they are "not wise," the Bible says. Liquor kills ten thousand people for every one person killed by a mad dog, yet we **shoot** the dog and **license** the liquor! That really doesn't make sense.

Young people, stop and think before you drug or drink.

II. AVOID A LIFE OF STRIFE; OBEY YOUR PARENTS WHO GAVE YOU LIFE

You are an extension of your parents. People judge them by the way you act and react. Whether you know it or not, everybody judges your home and family by the way you act and react in the schoolroom, at church, on the playground—everywhere. Some of you wonder how such **dull** parents ever produced such a **bright** child! Paul says in Ephesians 6:2: *"Honour thy father and mother."* Proverbs 30:17 contains a very stern warning about being disrespectful to parents: "The eye that mocketh at his father, and despiseth to obey his mother, the ravens of the valley shall pick it out, and the young eagles shall eat it." If I see an eyeball in the mouth of a raven, I will know that somebody had disrespect for Mama or Daddy. This is a serious warning.

When parents get older, infirm and sick, many sons and daughters ignore them. That is a tragedy, a sin before God. It doesn't matter how old or feeble they are: honor them, take care of them, and do for them what they can't do for themselves. They have been doing for you all of your lives. Now don't neglect them in their old age. Don't let your parents down; they brought you up!

III. BE HUMBLE ENOUGH TO OBEY; ONE DAY YOU WILL BE GIVING ORDERS

If you think you are smarter than the teacher or the pastor or the youth leader, wait a minute! You had better watch it, for one day you will be in the position of giving other people orders. Ephesians 6:1 says, "Children [including young people], obey your parents in the Lord: for this is right." An old adage goes like this: He who cannot **obey** cannot **command.** If you don't learn to obey, others are not going to obey you. Obedience speaks of love, respect, honor and admiration. The degree to which you respect your parents will be the degree to which you obey them.

Children, young people, be humble enough to obey your parents in the Lord.

IV. TURN AWAY FROM UNCLEAN THINKING

Proverbs 23:7 reads, "For as he thinketh in his heart, so is he." Your thoughts, the things you sit around thinking about, will one day become your deeds. What you think, you will do. You are not what you **think** you are, but what you **think,** you **are.** Look at this scriptural admonition in Philippians 4:8, 9:

"Finally, brethren, whatsoever things are true [not untrue], *whatsoever things are honest* [not dishonest], *whatsoever things are just* [not unjust], *whatsoever things are pure* [not impure], *whatsoever things are lovely* [not unlovely], *whatsoever things are of good report* [not a bad report]; *if there be any virtue, and if there be any praise, think on these things."*

Think positive thoughts. Think clean thoughts.

I would like to imagine that in every one of us is a little weaver sitting inside weaving cloth. This little weaver uses certain kinds of threads in your heart, in your life, in your soul. He sits weaving all day long. If you think bad thoughts, he uses a dark colored thread; if you think good thoughts, he uses gold and silver threads to make the character that one day you will be—simply because of the way you **think**.

Avoid evil thoughts. Learn to think good thoughts.

V. DON'T SHOW OFF
WHILE DRIVING

If you want to race, go to Indianapolis. Don't race on the freeways or byways. "His fuel was rich; his speed was high; he parked in a ditch to watch the curve go by." Some of you have already had that experience. If you get out on the public streets to show your stuff, they will shovel you up and take you to a hospital or to the morgue. I am warning you: don't act foolish behind the wheel.

A definition: "A tree is a huge vegetable that stands by the road for fifty years, then all of a sudden jumps out in front of a teenage driver." Some good advice: you will use your **horn** less if you use your **head** more.

If you are determined to be the speedster of the community, remember the following:

When doing 45 miles an hour, sing, "Highways Are Handy Ways."

When you reach 55, sing, "I'm But a Stranger Here; Heaven Is My Home."

At 65 sing, "When the Roll Is Called Up Yonder."

When you do 75, sing, "Nearer My God to Thee."

At 85 sing, "Lord, I'm Coming Home."

Someone has said, "Some cars have **fluid** drive; others just have a **drip** behind the wheel." Here is some good advice given by another: "Always drive so your **license** will expire before **you** do."

Drive carefully. Remember, if you want to race, go to Indianapolis Speedway.

VI. MAKE SURE YOUR DATE WOULD MAKE A GOOD MATE

Some of you guys have big problems. Your biggest is finding a girl **pretty** enough to please you and **dumb** enough to date you. You heard about the girl who sent her picture away to the "Lonely Hearts Club"; it was sent back with a little note: "We are not this lonely." Beauty is only skin deep and fades quickly; character lasts forever.

Young men and young women, don't say, "I'll date anybody I want to. I don't care what Mama or Daddy says; I don't care what the pastor or youth director says." This is just a very innocent and simple and temporary thing. But wait a minute! Something begins to happen—a feeling like nothing you have ever felt before. The first thing you know, you are involved with somebody you really didn't want to be involved with.

When the old heartstrings begin to tie in, be careful!

Love at first sight never happens before breakfast! My mother used to say, "Son, if you can stand them before breakfast, you can probably take them all day long." Until sixteen a boy is a "boy scout." When he turns sixteen, he becomes a "girl scout." Some of you started scouting long before then!

Be careful: you have all of your life to live with him or with her.

Love is a funny thing—
  It's just like a lizard:
It curls up around your heart
  And jumps into your gizzard.

Love is like an onion—
  We taste it with delight:
But when it's gone,
  We wonder what ever made us bite.

Love is swell.
    It's so enticing.
  It's orange jell.
      It's strawberry icing.

It's chocolate mousse.
It's roasted goose.
It's ham on rye.
It's banana pie.
Love's all good things without a question.
In other words—it's indigestion!

A young fellow says, "She is so sweet, I could just eat her up!" Ten years from now, you will wish you had! Be careful in choosing a **date**: that one may become your **mate**.

VII. ATTEND CHURCH ON A REGULAR BASIS

I cannot stress too much the importance of regular

church attendance. Church can give you in your life what you can't get at school or at the clubs or at your organizations or at your little societies. All of those are good, but church and doing God's will are more important than anything else.

When you are faithful in church attendance and live morally, you are saying to everyone, "I want to do God's will; I have dedicated my life to Christ." We don't dedicate ourselves to a program; we dedicate ourselves to a **Person**—Christ.

VIII. DON'T CULTIVATE SLEAZY FRIENDSHIPS; YOUR FRIENDS REFLECT YOU

You are likely to become what they are. Many times I have had parents say to me, "My son knows better; he just got with the wrong crowd." So don't get with the wrong crowd! Be willing to stand alone, and you will not be alone, because Jesus will stand with you. It may mean drawing a dividing line, a line of spiritual demarcation. You may have to put some of your friends on the other side of that line and tell them, "I'm on this side, and I'm going to stay on this side because this is where my line is spiritually."

Do your best to influence and win your associates to Christ, but don't let them drag you down. It doesn't take much pulling for that to happen, either. How many rotten apples does it take to spoil a whole barrel of apples? Just one. So be careful. Look at this warning, this admonition, from Proverbs 1:10–18:

"My son, if sinners entice thee, consent thou not.

"If they say, Come with us, let us lay wait for blood, let us lurk privily for the innocent without cause:

"Let us swallow them up alive as the grave; and whole, as those that go down into the pit:

117

"We shall find all precious substance, we shall fill our houses with spoil:

"Cast in thy lot among us; let us all have one purse:

"My son, walk not thou in the way with them; refrain thy foot from their path:

"For their feet run to evil, and make haste to shed blood.

"Surely in vain the net is spread in the sight of any bird.

"And they lay wait for their own blood; they lurk privily for their own lives."

What is all that saying? Out there at school, on the playground, when the crowd that is up to nothing good comes along and says to you, "Come on and go with us, take a ride with us," don't do it! Don't cast your lot with them. Don't become a part of those who are up to no good. They will promise you, "Come on, we can really have everything we want. All we have to do is knock off one store or rob one bank."

You say, "But, Preacher, nobody has ever pulled that on me." Tomorrow somebody can influence you to do that if you don't **pray** like you ought and **stay** where you ought to **stay**. It happens every day. Good fellows, good girls, good guys get with the wrong crowd, get caught up in the euphoria of it all; and the first thing you know, they have stolen or robbed or even murdered.

Proverbs 22:24 says (and this is the crux of it), "Make no friendship with an angry man; and with a furious man thou shalt not go." Be careful about your companions.

IX. AVOID FOLLOWING THE CROWD

Be an engine, not a caboose. Don't let anybody lead you around. You be out front. Mob psychology takes over when you get with a crowd. People in a crowd say and do things that they would never say or do alone. But because they are in a crowd, they lose inhibition and go with the flow.

Don't get caught up in mob psychology. An unorganized crowd is a mob, whatever else you call them. That is what happened in Los Angeles. I rather doubt that many of those people really intended to do what they did. They wouldn't have done it if there had been just one or two of them; but when hundreds began running in the street, they were willing to go out and rob stores, pull out televisions, shoot people and set buildings on fire. They did it all because mob psychology took over.

Don't get caught up in that kind of crowd. Stay away from it. Be your own person. There is not much **individuality** anymore. We take on the flavor, the color, the thinking, the thought processes of those around us. Let's take on the thought processes of God. Be your own person in Christ.

> **Be your own person in Christ.**

X. GOVERN YOUR LIFE BY GOD'S COMMANDMENTS

This is by far the most important of all. Listen to the original Ten Commandments. Learn them, love them, live by them. They are listed in Exodus 20:1–17:

"And God spake all these words, saying,

"I am the LORD *thy God, which have brought thee out of the land of Egypt, out of the house of bondage.*

"Thou shalt have no other gods before me.

"Thou shalt not make unto thee any graven image, or any likeness of any thing that is in heaven above, or that is in the earth beneath, or that is in the water under the earth.

"Thou shalt not bow down thyself to them, nor serve them: for I the LORD thy God am a jealous God, visiting the iniquity of the fathers upon the children unto the third and fourth generation of them that hate me;

"And shewing mercy unto thousands of them that love me, and keep my commandments.

"Thou shalt not take the name of the LORD thy God in vain; for the LORD will not hold him guiltless that taketh his name in vain.

"Remember the sabbath day, to keep it holy.

"Six days shalt thou labour, and do all thy work:

"But the seventh day is the sabbath of the LORD thy God: in it thou shalt not do any work, thou, nor thy son, nor thy daughter, thy manservant, nor thy maidservant, nor thy cattle, nor thy stranger that is within thy gates:

"For in six days the LORD made heaven and earth, the sea, and all that in them is, and rested the seventh day: wherefore the LORD blessed the sabbath day, and hallowed it.

"Honour thy father and thy mother: that thy days may be long upon the land which the LORD thy God giveth thee.

"Thou shalt not kill.

"Thou shalt not commit adultery.

"Thou shalt not steal.

"Thou shalt not bear false witness against thy neighbour.

"Thou shalt not covet thy neighbour's house, thou shalt not covet thy neighbour's wife, nor his manservant, nor his maidservant, nor his ox, nor his ass, nor any thing that is thy neighbour's."

These are God's Ten Commandments—commands written by the finger of Almighty God.

I appeal to you to dedicate your life to Christ, and He will make it worth living.

ENEMIES THAT ATTACK THE CHRISTIAN HOME

"So shall they fear the name of the LORD from the west, and his glory from the rising of the sun. When the enemy shall come in like a flood, the Spirit of the LORD shall lift up a standard against him."—Isa. 59:19.

The enemy is the Devil, Satan, the adversary, Apollyon, the destroyer, the deceiver, the liar, the accuser of the brethren. At this very moment Satan is accusing us before God. He accused Job. He tried to make God turn against Job. He is doing the same thing against you and me. Make no mistake about it, Public Enemy Number One is on a rampage in the world, and he is no respecter of persons. He is out to destroy us. It matters not where we live, what our status is, nor our financial base, nor how long we have been Christians, nor how strong we are in the Faith; Satan is on a rampage, and he doesn't care whom he hurts. He is forceful, fearless and forward; he is pernicious, persistent and powerful; he is deceptive, diabolical and demeaning; and he is out to get us.

I am glad the Bible says, "Greater is he that is in you, than he that is in the world." Not like a ripple, but like a flood, the enemy comes against God's people.

Do you know what the Devil's goal is? He is not out after the government *per se*. He is not really out after the church as such. The Devil's goal is to disturb and destroy the home and everything having to do with God, with righteousness and with holiness. Acts 13:10 describes him as the enemy of all righteousness. The Devil's ambition is to become like God.

Satan's "I Will's"

In Isaiah, chapter 14, are five "I will's" of Satan. There are only two philosophies in life to follow. One is the philosophy of Jesus, who, in the Garden of Gethsemane, prayed, "Not my will, but thine, be done." The other is the philosophy of Satan who said, "I will" five times in Isaiah 14. In verses 13 and 14 Satan said, "I will ascend into heaven, I will exalt my throne above the stars of God: I will sit also upon the mount of the congregation, in the sides of the north: I will ascend above the heights of the clouds; I will be like the most High." That is Satan's philosophy. Young people, when you say, "I will do my own thing," without regarding what anybody else thinks, or what the Bible says, or what the pastor says, or what parents say, you are following the Devil. You have incorporated his philosophy in your life, and that philosophy heads downward to destruction, to despair and right into the clutches of Hell. Don't say, "I will," unless you are saying you will do whatever God wills for you to do.

Know who your enemy is so you will recognize him when you see him. The Devil is the pernicious one, the diabolical one, the deceptive one, and he is alive and doing well.

> **The Devil's number one target is the home.**

The Devil's number one target is not the government, not industry, not business, not the school and not the church. The Devil's number one target is the home, the basic unit of society. As goes the home, so go the church, the educational program, the business program, the governmental program and all other programs. It all begins in the **home**.

Shame on you parents who "send" your children to Sunday school! Shame on you parents who bring your children to Sunday school, throw them in the classroom and say to the teacher and pastor in so many words, "You take care of them. You teach them. I don't have time to fool with them."

Sadly enough, all of the spiritual instruction that many children get is in the Sunday school class, AWANAs or the training time, even though their parents are sitting on the pew every Sunday. That is sad.

Do you want to know what's wrong with your children? Look in the mirror. We dress ourselves up and pretend. Listen! Painting the pump doesn't purify the water. We have a great deal of showcase dressing but not much on the shelf. God help us!

Satan's Strategy

If the Devil can destroy the Christian **home**, he can impede the progress of the **church**. If he can impede the progress of the **church**, he can weaken the structure of the **nation**. If he can weaken the structure of the **nation**, he can destroy the foundation of **democracy**.

The awesome, sobering question is asked in Psalm 11:3: "If the foundations be destroyed, what can the righteous do?" If we allow the Devil to destroy our homes, to break up our marriages, to distract us from God, we weaken the very fiber of our nation, to say nothing of the fiber of our churches.

Let me make this declaration: Within the framework of the moral and spiritual values of the home lie the strength and stability of the church; within the strength and stability of the church lies the hope of the nation.

Three Homes

There are three homes that every Christian ought to have: first, an **earthly** home. There is no place like home. After having fought the world and the Devil all day and problems on the job, you want to go home and shut it all out for awhile. Everybody needs an **earthly** home.

Second, everybody needs a **church** home, a place where you can say, "These are my people; this is my church home; this is my pastor; these are my fellow members."

Third, everybody needs a **heavenly** home.

> My heavenly home is bright and fair;
> No pain nor death shall enter there.
>
> If you get there before I do,
> Just look for me; I'm coming too.

This chapter is titled "Enemies That Attack the Christian Home." The Christian home is being attacked by

SATANIC FORCES FROM BELOW

"Be sober, be vigilant; because your adversary the devil, as a roaring lion, walketh about, seeking whom he may devour:

"Whom resist stedfast in the faith, knowing that the same afflictions are accomplished in your brethren that are in the world."—I Pet. 5:8, 9.

Satanic efforts from below, demonic forces, are attacking our homes. Demonic forces operate effectively when God's people submit to Satan's authority.

Your life is being governed either by Jesus Christ or by Satan. You are following either the Lord's precepts, promises and philosophy of life, or Satan's. Sadly enough, many Christians are submitting to the authority of the Devil more than they are to the authority of God. The Devil will make his appeal sound so good. He so sugarcoats the bitter pill of death, destruction, Hell and damnation that many Christians swallow it without a drink of water. He is conniving and scheming, and the moment we agree with him, we are in serious trouble.

Many people intend to go to church, but the Devil

comes along and says to them, "You have only one day a week in which to sleep late. You have to get up early every morning. Why don't you just lie here and rest?" You listen and do what you wanted to do all along—miss the services. Then when heartache and problems and trials come and the family is scattered to the winds, you wonder, *Why didn't the church do something for me?* The church can't do it all. The Sunday school can't do it all. The pastor can't do it all. You have to do something for yourself.

The Devil is out to destroy our families, and there are seven demons that he is throwing against us every day.

1. **The demon of discouragement.** If the Devil can get Mother and Daddy discouraged about the church, that will destroy the whole family program.

2. **The demon of depression.** More people are suffering from depression these days than at any other time in history. We take pills to get us up in the morning; we take pills to get us through the day; we take pills to put us to sleep at night; we take pills again the next morning. The psychologists and psychiatrists tell us the number one problem is depression. Depression is a demon from Hell trying to destroy the people of God.

3. **The demon of despondency.**

4. **The demon of despair.**

5. **The demon of deficiency.**

6. **The demon of doubt.** If the Devil can get you to doubt that what you are doing is right, doubt your salvation, doubt the Word of God, doubt the reality of God, doubt Jesus Christ, he has you right where he wants you.

7. **The demon of defeat.**

It all starts with discouragement. If the Devil can get the family discouraged, he will get them depressed; he will get them despondent; he will take them through the valley of despair; he will put them in a place of deficiency; he will get them to doubt; then he will defeat them. The strongest family can be defeated if seven demons are on top of it.

> Jesus was revealed to destroy the power of Satan.

What is our defense? "When the enemy shall come in like a flood, the Spirit of the LORD shall lift up a standard against him." Jesus was revealed to destroy the power of Satan.

Now look at I John 3:8: "He that committeth sin is of the devil; for the devil sinneth from the beginning. For this purpose the Son of God was manifested, that he might destroy the works of the devil." There is a satanic attack from below against the home. Demons all over this world are trying to destroy and defeat God's people.

The Christian home is being attacked by

SUBTLE FORCES FROM WITHIN

Sometimes that which happens within is worse than that which happens without. A warning: Some good Christian families are sowing the seeds of their own destruction and probably don't realize that it is happening. Paul says to young Timothy in II Timothy 3:1–7:

"This know also, that in the last days perilous times shall come.

"For men shall be lovers of their own selves, covetous, boasters, proud, blasphemers, disobedient to parents, unthankful, unholy,

"Without natural affection, trucebreakers, false accusers, incontinent, fierce, despisers of those that are good,

"Traitors, heady, highminded, lovers of pleasures more than lovers of God;

"Having a form of godliness, but denying the power thereof: from such turn away.

"For of this sort are they which creep into houses, and lead captive silly women laden with sins, led away with divers lusts,

"Ever learning, and never able to come to the knowledge of the truth."

The Apostle Paul lists a whole catalogue of evils here: covetousness, selfishness, boasters, proud, blasphemers; and "disobedient to parents" is listed among these cardinal sins. Disobedience to parents is listed along with sins like lying, the breaking of truces, being proud, homosexuality and incest.

One of the greatest sins is incest. Can you imagine a man sexually abusing his own daughter! Or a mother having an incestuous relationship with her own son!

Right in the middle of these Paul lists categories of evil—unnatural affection, homosexuality, rape, murder, lying, cheating, stealing—"disobedient to parents." May God have mercy on America, the so-called "nation under God"! We have only one defense against all of this—the Word of God. Look at II Timothy 3:12–15:

"Yea, and all that will live godly in Christ Jesus shall suffer persecution.

"But evil men and seducers shall wax worse and worse, deceiving, and being deceived.

"But continue thou in the things which thou hast learned and hast been assured of, knowing of whom thou hast learned them;

"And that from a child thou hast known the holy scriptures, which are able to make thee wise unto salvation through faith which is in Christ Jesus."

The only defense is the Word of God. The Apostle Paul gives us a serious warning: 'Take heed of the things you have learned from the Word of God, lest at any moment you let them slip away from you.'

Let me illustrate. Here is the Word of God. I lay it on the desk. The Bible is not going to move; but if I keep backing away from where the Bible is, I am getting further and further away from the Word of God. The Bible is still there, the Truth is still there, God is still there, principles are still there, but I have slipped away. The Bible hasn't moved. That is what is happening. The Bible is where it has always been. Paul says, 'Let me warn you: take heed that you don't slip away from those things that you have learned.'

I hear people say, "I want a new experience." They don't need a new experience; they need to remember what they already know. They need to keep in mind what they have already learned—the basic, fundamental principles of righteousness, holiness, purity, morality, godliness and biblical living.

We don't need a new experience; we need a revival of the old-time religion in our hearts, in our lives and in our homes!

The Christian home is being attacked by

SEDUCTIVE FORCES FROM WITHOUT

We read in Ephesians 6:10–18:

"Finally, my brethren, be strong in the Lord, and in the power of his might.

"Put on the whole armour of God, that ye may be able to stand against the wiles of the devil.

"For we wrestle not against flesh and blood, but against principalities, against powers, against the rulers of the darkness of this world, against spiritual wickedness in high places.

"Wherefore take unto you the whole armour of God, that ye may be able to withstand in the evil day, and having done all, to stand.

"Stand therefore, having your loins girt about with truth, and

having on the breastplate of righteousness;

"And your feet shod with the preparation of the gospel of peace;

"Above all, taking the shield of faith, wherewith ye shall be able to quench all the fiery darts of the wicked.

"And take the helmet of salvation, and the sword of the Spirit, which is the word of God:

"Praying always with all prayer and supplication in the Spirit, and watching thereunto with all perseverance and supplication for all saints."

We are in a battle. The forces of evil have arrayed themselves against God and His people. Verse 11 mentions "the wiles of the devil." *Wile* means "an attempt to lure as by a magic spell"—an attempt by Satan to lure you away from God, putting you under a magic spell of some kind.

The Devil can so paralyze us spiritually and so deceive us that we will think we are doing right, when we are only under his magic, under his spell. Paul warns us to watch out for the wiles of the Devil. He deceives, he beguiles, he tricks. He has no difficulty making sin look innocent. He uses everything in his arsenal to entice young people away from God, the church, the home, and from the basic principles of the Word of God.

Thirty-six years ago, in 1962, the Supreme Court of the United States of America declared there would be no more prayer in the public schools. What has happened? Statistics reveal that the morality level has gone down, down, down in the public school. Take God and the Bible out, and there is nothing left. History proves that. We have discharged God from the army, we have expelled Him from the classroom, and about the only place a young person can find Him now is in jail. They will let you take the Bible into jails but not into schools. Because the word *Christmas* has the word *Christ* in it, the ruling came in Colorado, "You cannot put up any banner that has *Christmas* on it." It is illegal to mention the name of Christ in public schools. Many teachers do it, but if it were brought to court, they would be ruled against. Statistics are frightening.

> Since the court excluded religious principles from students at schools, premarital sexual activity among 15-year-old students has increased almost five hundred percent, with half of the sexually active males having had their first sexual experience between the ages of 11 and 13.

> Sexually transmitted diseases have increased over two hundred percent, and teenage student pregnancies have increased over four hundred percent, causing the United States to become the Western world's leader in teenage pregnancies, with one and a quarter million adolescent pregnancies each year.

These statistics do not come from a foreign country where they don't even acknowledge God. This is happening in the good old USA. Since God was expelled from the classroom, it has been deteriorating—going down, down, down. Mentally, intellectually, morally, socially—in every way the public educational system has gone down. Romans 1 states that when individuals do not "retain God in their knowledge," they become filled with every kind of wickedness: murder, strife, malice, etc.

Observe the reality in the following news article:

> Student violence is now a troublesome problem facing America's schools. At most of the Oakland, California unified school district's 92 schools, the fight against crime and violence is unending. A semiautomatic rifle with fifteen hollow-point bullets was among the weapons confiscated by district

officials within the last year.

Franklin Elementary School, trying to ensure that students know how to hit the ground when bullets fly, carries out shooting drills twice a year.

On the average, a Detroit child was shot every day in 1986 in the public schools of the city of Detroit. Parents are demanding metal detectors and searches for weapons, and officials said they would resume weapons searches in the schools. "I'm tired of kids carrying guns like they used to take a lunch," Mayor Coleman Young said.

A new security program that brought 150 police officers into the Chicago public schools resulted in an unprecedented 4,306 arrests on the school premises in the first four months of this school year. Police made nearly fourteen times the number of drug arrests as had been made in the previous fall, and nearly twelve times the weapons arrests. There were 1,122 arrests for disorderly conduct, 910 for battery, 738 for criminal trespass and 229 for alleged weapons violations.

Currently, 5,200 high school teachers are attacked by students every month, and one-fifth of them require medical treatment. Additionally, the National Institute of Education's Safe School Study reveals only seventeen to nineteen percent of violent offenses against urban youths, 12-15 years of age, occur in the street. Sixty-eight percent of the robberies and fifty percent of the assaults on youngsters of this age occur at school. An estimated 282,000 secondary school students reported that they were attacked at school in a typical one-month period. The risk of violence to teenagers is greater in public schools than elsewhere.

An article in the September 9, 1990, *Fort Worth Star Telegram* revealed the current trend in student fashions.

> Bullet-proof back-to-school clothes are the latest thing for children who run a dangerous gauntlet to and from class. School blazers and other jackets are fitted with 129 bullet-resistant pads. Added shielding from flying bullets can be had from a bullet-proof book bag or clipboards.

Bullet-proof back-to-school clothes! From without, we are being attacked by subtle forces. The Devil is on his last round.

THREE FORMIDABLE ENEMIES ARE TRIPLE TROUBLE

Hard rock music is the first of the triplets. That is at the base of most of the violence, because these hard rock songs have lyrics that most parents know nothing about. You had better start listening because they are encouraging sex, homosexuality, crime, violence and all the rest of such stuff in the songs. They are seductive, subtle and satanic. No Christian home ought to allow rock music in it. It is dangerous. It feeds children's minds and their souls, and it poisons them. Ask some fellows who have gone down that road; they will tell you that listening to hard rock started them into drugs, illicit sex and crime. Now look at their lives. It all started by listening to rock music.

Why would anybody pay twenty-five or thirty dollars to see a bunch of idiots jump up and down and twist their spines to the point that they will suffer for years to come? Why listen to their loud music? When I drive down the street, I can't even hear the horn blow or listen to a radio program because some nut has pulled up by me playing loud rock music.

You say, "It won't happen to us." It is happening right in the homes of Christian parents. Get the rock music out. Don't give it away. Don't put that poison on somebody else. Burn it. It is dangerous. It is damnable. For your own good, get that rock music out of your home!

Sexual involvement is the second of the triplets. What a danger! Condoms—now being passed out in public schools! "Safe sex"—what a tragedy! How low can we reach! Why don't they teach children what the Bible teaches on sex?

I appreciate what the baseball star Nolan Ryan said in the local paper: "I don't understand the media making a hero out of a man who has admitted he now has AIDS because he slept with hundreds of women." Why would we make a hero out of a guy like that? Why would our government pay three hundred thousand dollars to decide which picture of Elvis Presley to put on a postage stamp? That doesn't make sense. If you are an Elvis fan, God forgive you! Such rock and roll music has damned more students, more families, more hearts, more homes than any other one thing. "The King of Rock and Roll"! God have mercy on America when we make guys like him our heroes, or the basketball player Magic Johnson who got AIDS from promiscuous living. To the media I say, quit playing him up as a hero to our young people. "If he hadn't been promiscuous, he wouldn't have AIDS" is what the media ought to say.

Young people, the only safe way is abstinence. Sex is sacred, reserved for marriage only. And for God's sake, and for your sake, keep it that way.

The third triplet is drug abuse. The number one drug in America is alcohol. Don't try to convince your sons and daughters of the dangers of cocaine while you sip your beer. Alcohol is wrong, drugs are wrong, illicit sex is wrong, rock music is wrong. To survive, we must right this wrong, live like Christians and act like Christians.

CONCLUSION

Five things you parents can do to build a fence of protective love around your home:

- Know **what** your kids **listen** to.
- Know **whom** your kids **associate** with.
- Know **where** your kids go.
- Know **what time** they go **out** and **what time** they come **in**.
- Know **what** they **take with them** and **what** they **bring home**.

The only hope for the home is an **umbrella** of divine protection.

THE SANCTITY OF
THE HOME

"Wives, submit yourselves unto your own husbands, as unto the Lord.

"For the husband is the head of the wife, even as Christ is the head of the church: and he is the saviour of the body.

"Therefore as the church is subject unto Christ, so let the wives be to their own husbands in every thing.

"Husbands, love your wives, even as Christ also loved the church, and gave himself for it;

"That he might sanctify and cleanse it with the washing of water by the word,

"That he might present it to himself a glorious church, not having spot, or wrinkle, or any such thing; but that it should be holy and without blemish.

"So ought men to love their wives as their own bodies. He that loveth his wife loveth himself.

"For no man ever yet hated his own flesh; but nourisheth and cherisheth it, even as the Lord the church:

"For we are members of his body, of his flesh, and of his bones.

"For this cause shall a man leave his father and mother, and shall be joined unto his wife, and they two shall be one flesh.

"This is a great mystery: but I speak concerning Christ and the church.

"Nevertheless let every one of you in particular so love his wife even as himself; and the wife see that she reverence her husband."—
Eph. 5:22–33.

If we would build our lives, our homes and our marriages by the prescription God gives us here, we would have happy homes. A great number of books have been written on the home and on family relationships. I am certainly not denigrating these books; but the longer I live, the more I deal with people's problems, and the more I see of raw humanity, the more I am convinced that the Word of God has the answers to those problems, those perils, those difficulties, those trials and those heartaches that we have in our individual lives, in our homes, in our churches, in our businesses, on our jobs, in the nation and in the world. An old Chinese proverb says:

> If there is righteousness in the heart,
> There will be beauty in the character.
>
> If there is beauty in the character,
> There will be harmony in the home.
>
> If there is harmony in the home,
> There will be order in the nation.
>
> If there is order in the nation,
> There will be peace in the world.

The **home** plays a vital role in the affairs of the world. Every area of life—government, politics, business, the economy, education—is affected by what happens in the home. He was right who said, "As goes the home, so goes the nation." He was right who said, "The hand that rocks the cradle rules the world."

The home didn't just spring up yesterday or in the last century. It is the oldest institution known to man. The home was in existence before the church was in existence. The home existed before there was a government. The home existed before there was ever a system of education. The home is the basic unit of society, and all else stems from the home. I cannot emphasize too much the importance of your home.

The home is the **flagship** of morality in our nation. The morals that govern the home will ultimately govern the community. The home is the **cornerstone** of democracy. No nation is any stronger than the homes that make it up. The home is the **bulwark** of society—the **pillar** upon which all social affairs are built. The home is the **backbone** of Christianity. The church is what the homes make it, nothing more and nothing less.

Let me slip into your home for a moment, draw the curtain back and look on what is happening. Show me the **books** you read, the **entertainment** you engage in, the kind of **music** you listen to, the **movies** you watch, the **language** you speak, and I will tell you the moral and spiritual temperature of your home.

The Greek word for *home* means "a shrine for the gods." Little wonder that Jesus said to Zacchaeus, "To day I must abide at thy house." Jesus Christ deserves a place in your home. He should be the unseen Guest at every meal. He is the **only** One who can straighten out your marital problems. The psychologist, the counselor, the psychiatrist, the pastor and your friends can contribute, but **only** in Christ will you find the solutions.

FUNCTION OF THE HOME

The function of the home is threefold. It is **biological**, the reproduction through the birth of offspring. It is **sociological**. The first social contact that a child has is within the framework of his home. It is a little society within itself. In the home social mores are learned at an early age. It is **theological**. Early in life, patterns of behavior, manners, deportment and conduct are learned in the home. So the function of the home is biological, sociological and theological.

Biblical instruction must begin at home. Listen to what God says through Moses in Deuteronomy 6:6–9:

> **Biblical instruction must begin at home.**

"And these words, which I command thee this day, shall be in thine heart:

"And thou shalt teach them diligently unto thy children, and shalt talk of them when thou sittest in thine house, and when thou walkest by the way, and when thou liest down, and when thou risest up.

"And thou shalt bind them for a sign upon thine hand, and they shall be as frontlets between thine eyes.

"And thou shalt write them upon the posts of thy house, and on thy gates."

Many books have been written on "how to"—"How to raise children," "How to be a good husband," "How to be a good wife," "How to have a happy family." These all contribute, but the one Book that gives us divinely inspired principles is the Bible. Don't ever say, "Well, that passage was in the Old Testament, and those principles were for yesteryear. This is 1998." Yes, it is 1998, but we need the principles of yesteryear in the decade of the nineties.

If we try to keep up with the spirit of this world, if we try to follow the precepts of modern psychology, modern psychiatry and modern counseling, we are in trouble. Unless it is based upon the Word of God, it is not worthy of our time, it will not answer our questions, and it will not provide the solution to any or all of our problems. We must get back to the Bible. We must get on our faces before God and beg Him to give insight, foresight, proper perspective and wisdom.

You believe God is a gentleman. You believe God means what He says in James 1:5: "If any of you lack wisdom, let him ask of God, that giveth to all men liberally, and upbraideth not; and it shall be given him." Moses said, 'When you get up in the morning, when you walk during the day, when you lie down at night, write it on the doorposts.' The Bible has the answers to the perplexing problems that confront us in this century.

This is a mad, mixed-up world. Satan is insidiously creeping into homes, schools, churches, organizations, government and politics, bent on destroying the foundations of truth. The only thing that will defeat Satan (Jesus proved this in His temptation) is the Word of God: "It is written."

The church can provide basic biblical knowledge for your children, but it cannot mold the character of your children. The church is totally helpless to do anything without the full support and cooperation of parents. Don't blame the church if you are taking issue with the pastor, the youth pastor and with the rules and regulations of the church. When your children go wrong, don't blame the church. There must be a cooperation, a togetherness, a walking together. "Can two walk together, except they be agreed?"

The church has based its principles and practices on the Word of God, and the home must conform to those principles and practices. Don't cause friction by criticizing when the church tries to keep your children in the straight and narrow way. Abide by it. Those in leadership at the church have the best interest of your children at heart. We are trying to help you parents bring up your children in the fear and nurture and admonition of the Lord.

An article in a newspaper some years ago was entitled "First Aid for Ailing Houses," a "how-to" message: how to repair the plumbing, how to repair the electricity, how to repair the roof, how to repair the foundation. But the problem is not ailing **houses**; it is ailing **homes**. There is a difference. The main difference between a house and a home is a four-letter word spelled L-O-V-E. A house is built by hands; a home is built by **hearts**.

> **A home is built by hearts.**

Victor Hugo said,

A house is built of logs and stone, of tiles and posts and piers.
A home is built of loving deeds that last a thousand years.

John Payne put it this way: "Be it ever so humble, there's no place like home."

THE HOME IS SACRED

There are four reasons why the home is a sacred institution:

God ordained the home. The home is sacred because God ordained it. There is a great deal of talk about open marriages, plural marriages, trial marriages or no marriage at all. However, the Bible gives a formula for marriage, and it began in the Garden with Adam and Eve (not Adam and Steve). Why would two males go to a courthouse to get a license to get married? The first command that God gives to families is to reproduce, and two males or two females cannot reproduce. Even if we didn't have Scripture against homosexuality and lesbianism, common sense would teach us better. God brought together the first man and the first woman. God created man, and man was in the world by himself. Then God made the woman. Poor Eve didn't have much of a choice! It was Adam or nobody!

It reminds me of the story of the old maid in church. The pastor said, "Now, I am going to let you choose your hymns for today." She stood up, looked over the congregation, and said, "I will take him, him and him!"

Genesis 2:21–24 gives us God's formula:

"And the LORD God caused a deep sleep to fall upon Adam, and he slept: and he took one of his ribs, and closed up the flesh instead thereof;

"And the rib, which the LORD God had taken from man, made he a woman, and brought her unto the man.

"And Adam said, This is now bone of my bones, and flesh of my flesh: she shall be called Woman, because she was taken out of Man.

"Therefore shall a man leave his father and his mother, and shall cleave unto his wife: and they shall be one flesh."

The woman was not taken out of man's head, so that he could rule over her. The woman was not taken out of his feet, so he might trample her underfoot. But the woman was taken out of his side and near his heart, that he might love and protect her. Wedlock is not a deadlock but a holy lock, and once it is locked, you are to throw away the key. It is strange that people spend months and months preparing for a wedding ceremony and only a few minutes preparing for a marriage. The wedding ceremony is designed to last a few moments; the marriage is **designed** to last a **lifetime.**

We all admit that this sea of matrimony gets a little stormy at times, but God provides a life jacket, a raft, a compass for serious sailors. When you get into a little trouble, don't say, "Well, I shouldn't have married her anyway; I'm just going to pack up and leave. I don't love her anymore." No! Live with her whether you love her or not. Your living with her is not contingent on whether you love her like you did when you got married. Your living with her is a covenant that you entered into when you said, "I will." In this modern age, when one little argument comes, she packs up and goes back to Mother, or he packs up and goes—somewhere. God put man and woman together until death part them.

When Henry Ford was celebrating his golden wedding anniversary, somebody asked him, "Mr. Ford, to what do you attribute your fifty years of marriage?" He answered, "I use the

> **The home is ordained by God.**

same formula that I use in making cars: I stick with one model." Not bad advice. The home is ordained by God.

God structured the home. The home is sacred because God structured it. There is much nonsensical talk these days about restructuring the home. We need to remember that God structured the home thousands of years ago. Modern science, modern technology, modern psychology, modern psychiatry and modern counseling cannot improve on God's plan.

The old maid said to her pastor, "Pastor, I want to get married. I have prayed and prayed and prayed for a husband, but to no avail. What else can I do?"

The kindhearted pastor, wanting to help her, said, "Well, my dear, the Bible says one man for one woman, and one woman for one man. That is God's plan, and you cannot improve on it."

"But, Pastor," she said, "I don't want to improve on it; I just want to get in on it."

Saying "I will" or "I do" is serious business. It has a divine structure to it; therefore, no one should go into it blindly. Paul tells us what God's divine structure is in I Corinthians 11:3, 8, 9:

> "But I would have you know, that the head of every man is Christ; and the head of the woman is the man; and the head of Christ is God....
>
> "For the man is not of the woman; but the woman of the man.
>
> "Neither was the man created for the woman; but the woman for the man."

How does Paul delineate God's outline and structure? Here it is: Christ is the head of the man; the man is the head of the woman. God the Father is head of all, because He is head over Christ, who is head over the man, who is head over the woman. There is the divine order, and when that order is reversed (and in many homes either the woman has taken the authority or the children have been elevated to a place of authority), confusion and chaos follow.

In some homes, Mother or Daddy asks the children, "Can we eat now?" "Is it time for us to eat?" "Is it all right if we go get in the car now?" That is ridiculous! There is a breakdown in authority, and that breakdown in authority will show up in the classroom, in the White House, in the courthouse, in the statehouse, in the workhouse.

Let's get it straight: Man is the head of the home, and the Bible says that woman is to be in subjection. "Wives, submit yourselves unto your own husbands, as unto the Lord. For the husband is the head of the wife, even as Christ is the head of the church....Husbands, love your wives, even as Christ also loved the church, and gave himself for it."

If a husband would fulfill his biblically ordained role of loving his wife as Christ loved the church, he would have very little trouble getting her to be in submission to him.

Does subjection mean that the husband cracks the whip and shouts, "You have to do this and do it this way"? Men, if every few days you have to say, "I am head of this home; I am king of this castle," chances are, you are not. This Scripture tells the father, the husband, that he is responsible to God for the spiritual leadership in the home. It is his responsibility to see that the home functions according to God's plan.

The home is structured to meet the needs of the family. God knew what He was doing.

The home is a **communications** center where the family talks together. Dad, when did you last call the family together and say, "We are going to have a little fireside chat. There are some things we need to talk about"? It would save many heartaches down the way if you would take time out of your busy schedule to get your family together, turn off the television, sit down and say, "Listen, we are going to talk over some things."

The home is a **prayer** center. Dad, when was the last time you got your family together and prayed with them?

> The home is a prayer center.

The home is a **planning** center. It is exciting for the family to sit down and all members plan what they want to do. Try it!

The home is a **love** center.

The home is a **recreational** center. It doesn't take all the fancy toys and other forms of entertainment to make a family happy. Develop things right in the home to occupy leisure time, then you will know where your children are. You won't have to wonder if they will get in at eleven or twelve or one. If your children go out, know **when** your children leave, **where** they go, **with whom** they go, **what time** they get back, and **what** they bring back with them.

The tragedy of all tragedies is that many families have lost sight of the sanctity of the home. Many mothers know more about mixing cocktails than mixing cornbread. Many fathers care more about drinking than disciplining. Many children, sadly enough, hear more profanity than prayer. Luther Burbank wisely said, "If we paid no more attention to our plants than we do our children, we would have a garden of weeds."

God has entrusted you with children, and what a responsibility! If your children have been rebellious and disobedient, don't think that people will always judge you by their actions. If you have a wayward daughter or a rebellious son, I assure you that your pastor loves you, and so do Christian friends. Nothing blesses a pastor's heart more than for little children to come up and hug him. Don't stop them; don't snatch them away and say, "Don't bother the pastor." Hugging their pastor is a precious moment to children. They need that, as well as for Mother and Daddy to caress them. "Hugs, not drugs."

Take time with your children. Teach them how to do things. Play with them, love them and share with them. If the time comes when they are not what they ought to be, you can call your pastor. He will have a sympathetic ear. He will do all he can to help you retrieve and win back their love and respect. Your grief is his grief, your sorrow his sorrow, your hurt his hurt.

God honored the home. The home is sacred because God honored it. There are three divinely ordained institutions, and God has given a specific honor to each of the three: the **home**, the **government** and the **church**. God honors the home.

First, He honors the home by comparing the relationship of husband and wife to that of Christ and the church. 'Husbands, love your wives. Wives, be in submission. As Christ is the Head of the church, so the husband is the head of the home.'

Second, Jesus didn't choose the synagogue in which to perform His first miracle. He performed the first recorded miracle in a home, at a wedding in Cana of Galilee, thereby putting His divine approval upon the family, upon the home, upon the wedding ceremony and upon the marriage altar.

Third, God honors the home by writing so much about it in the Bible. Read Proverbs, Ephesians, II Timothy and I Peter. Those and many other books in the Bible describe the function and order of the home.

The home is sacred because God honors it.

God gave the home a purpose. The home is sacred because God gave it a specific purpose to fulfill. God wants your home to be a **palace** of **peace**, not a **house** of **horrors**. Sadly enough, many homes have become armed camps. Mom and Dad fuss at each other, Dad fusses at the children, and the children fuss at each other. There are going to be squabbles and a few fights along the way, but if the friction is too great and the pressure too much, sooner or later somebody is going to get out and be gone.

God never intended the home to be broken and scattered. Sin has done this. God never intended for families to be divided. Sin has done this. God never intended for families to be lost. Sin has done this. God wants all the family to come into the ark of safety. Remember what God said to Noah: "Come thou and all thy house into the ark." Remember what Paul said to the Philippian jailor: "Believe on the Lord Jesus Christ, and thou shalt be saved, and thy house." God wants them all to be in.

These are busy days. Fathers and mothers go their **separate** ways, in **separate** cars, paid for by **separate** bank accounts. Latchkey children are left free to come and go as they please. The neighbor's house has become a place of refuge. The kitchen has become a fast-food shop. The den has become an entertainment center. The family car has become a taxi. We are so busy, so bogged down and so bothered.

You may be saying, "But, Pastor, you don't understand." Yes, I do understand. I understand that we have to curtail some things to put **first** things **first**. We have to give up some of these activities. We are not going to be able to attend every meeting, every club, every entertainment. We can't do all those things and bring up our children in the fear and admonition of the Lord. Something has to give.

| Put first things first. |

Nobody seems to have much time anymore for family togetherness. I remember as a child when we used to gather around the radio in our home. We listened to Fibber McGee and Mollie. We listened to the Johnson Family. We listened to Amos and Andy. Those programs were so great. Now you have to have a wide-screen, color television. I wish we could blacken all the screens of all the televisions for awhile. The thing that gets the most attention in the average home is the television set! When you get up, you turn it on; the last thing you do at night is turn it off. Any family togetherness now is the TV blaring some brainwashing propaganda, most of which is not fit for family entertainment. Garbage used to be just on cable, but it is now on mainline networks. It all adds up to the fact that we are sadly, tragically neglecting the God-given purpose for the home. The home is the place to honor God. The home is a place to find spiritual strength and to cultivate family fellowship.

There are four things necessary for family fellowship and strength: love, forgiveness, understanding and a listening ear.

The home is where you teach moral and doctrinal truths and Daddy is the leader. I warn you again: If you delegate your authority to the school, to the church, to the state, to Mother or to any other person or organization, you are violating God's divine plan, and it has disastrous consequences.

"How can I teach my children?" You can teach by **precept**, just taking down the Bible and having family devotions. That doesn't mean that you have to read so many books in the Bible every morning and so many books every night. Read a portion of the Word of God, and say to your children, "This is what God says about this." Let them ask questions. Children are full of them. By the time the average child is fifteen, he has asked five hundred thousand questions. Read the Bible to them in family devotions. Oh, a family **altar** would **alter** many a family. Teach them right out of the Word of God, line upon line, precept upon precept.

Then you can teach them by **example**. Lifestyle is the best teacher. Someone has said, "The parent's life is the child's copybook." That means that your child will do what he sees you do. If going to church on Wednesday night is important to you, he will think it important. If winning souls is important to you, your child will believe it is important. If tithing is important to you, he will believe it is important. If praying is important for you, your child will believe it is important. If you don't do these things, he will get the idea that they are not important. If serving God is important in your home and life, your child will catch on.

Let me conclude by giving you a formula for a happy home:

1. Establish a family altar.
2. Avoid family feuds.
3. Develop family projects.
4. Share family problems.
5. Discover family togetherness.
6. Pursue family goals.
7. Participate in family discussions.
8. Cultivate family fun.
9. Demonstrate family love.
10. Minimize family faults.
11. Keep family secrets confidential.
12. Exercise family authority.

One mother and daddy had no time for God or the church. She was too busy with social clubs, cocktail parties and other things. He was taken up with golfing, fishing and hunting. One day when Mother came home from one of her excursions, she called for her son, but he didn't answer. She called a second time. No answer. She called a third time. Still no answer. When she went upstairs to his room, she found the boy had taken the gun from his daddy's forbidden gun rack and killed himself. This suicide note was found by his body: "I would rather be dead than to live in a house without love and without God."

That sad, true story has been told over and over again. The number one cause of death among teenagers is suicide. Every day somewhere in this country thirteen teenagers take their own lives. The reason many teenagers commit suicide is that they are tired of living in a home where there is no love and where God is relegated to second place.

How sacred is the home? It is God's institution. He has entrusted us with it. Let us make it the best that we can. Remember, houses are built by hands; homes are built by hearts.